HENRY FIELDING

January 12 – March 6, 1987

"Henry Fielding?" [ca. 1750], attributed to Sir Joshua Reynolds
(17.2 × 11.3 cm.) *Courtesy of the British Library, Department of
Prints and Drawings*

NEW BOOKS BY FIELDING

An Exhibition of the Hyde Collection

Cambridge: THE HOUGHTON LIBRARY

January 12 — March 6, 1987

SOURCES OF THE EXHIBITS

Viscountess Eccles 2, 6 (1), 8–10, 12–15, 19–20, 23, 24 (1),
    27–28, 30 (2), 31, 33–35, 39–42, 47, 49, 52–53, 55,
    57, 59–60, 69, 70 (1), 71–75

Harvard College
    Source unknown 62
    H. Amory, in mem. D. F. Hyde 7
    William Bentinck-Smith 65
    Francis S. Blake 70 (2)
    Child Memorial Library 56
    Duplicates fd. 21
    By Exchange 16, 61
    W. B. O. Field 22
    Arthur Freeman 18
    L. M. Friedman 32
    Friends of the Library 50, 58
    Greenough fd. 48, 51
    S. B. Grimson 3
    Philip Hofer 24 (2)
    A. A. Houghton, Jr. 46
    H. S. Howe fd. 4
    Lincoln fd. 54
    A. Lowell fd. 45
    Mrs. James McBey 63
    J. B. Munn, in mem. L. de J. Harvard 44
    Norton fd. 26
    H. K. Oliver 6 (2)
    Norton Perkins 1, 30 (1, 3)
    C. H. Reisinger 43
    Shapleigh fd. 29 (2)
    Subscription fd. of 1902 68
    George Ticknor 29 (1)
    Treat fd. 64
    E. J. Wendell 17
    H. E. Widener 11

Andover Harvard 66–67

Harvard Law School 5

Wellesley College 25

Cornell University 36

Columbia University 34

Design & Production by Richard C. Bartlett & Deborah S. Davies

Copyright © 1987 by the President and Fellows of Harvard
College

Library of Congress Cataloguing-in-Publication Data

New Books by Fielding.

    Exhibition held at the Houghton Library, Jan. 12–Mar. 6,
1987.

    1. Fielding, Henry, 1707–1754—Bibliography—Exhibi-
tions. 2. Hyde Collection—Exhibitions. I. Houghton Library.
Z8293.72.N48 1987 [PR3456]   016.823'5   86–18595
ISBN 0–91463–001–6 (pbk.)

INTRODUCTION ஒ

The Hyde Collection was begun by a husband, Donald Hyde, who hoped his wife would extend her researches in Elizabethan drama to the eighteenth century. The perception of bibliographical analogies was exact: just as the origin of the "Pavier Quartos" of Shakespeare manifested itself in contemporary binding collections, so does the origin of Millar's reprint of the *Grub-Street Opera;* and Fielding's "bad octavos" pose some of the same textual conundrums as Shakespeare's bad quartos. But as we now know, his wife's real designs were on Johnson and Mrs. Thrale. Too bad for Fielding.

This is a scholar's collection, abounding in multiple copies, piracies, abridgments, translations and ana — over two hundred items in all, from which I have selected thirty-seven for exhibition. Inevitably, like all work on Fielding today, it was built in the shadow of Cross's *History of Henry Fielding,* and Don was amazingly successful in acquiring items "not in" that definitive bio-bibliography; and he spiked the punch with many stunning pieces in "collector's condition" — to say nothing of manuscripts. Still, his major interest was research, insofar as this can be separated from collecting, and this catalogue has been written in the same spirit, for use in teaching undergraduate classes at Harvard what a hand-printed book — especially a novel — "looks like" and why; to show the nearly invisible relationships between a text and what are a little misleadingly called its "accidentals"; and to suggest that "collector's condition" should be of interest to more than collectors.

My title is, of course, ironic. So long as we judge the truth of a text by it origins, no modern edition — critical or practical — can tell us anything "new"; for such revelations, we must turn to the past. On the other hand, we should not mistake first editions for "the originals" or "what the author actually wrote." They are only evidence, and to judge them rightly means to see their difference from what is familiar to us. They then become "new" in a very real sense, and so do our modern conventions.

"Bare is brotherless back" says the Icelandic proverb, and I have been generously protected by my brethren and sistren who read over early drafts: by Martin Battestin and John Lancaster, especially, who saved me from grievous errors; by Susan Staves, who brought a very human interest to my too-refined discipline; by Ruthe Battestin, who shared her bottomless research; by Roger Stoddard, who propped up my enterprise with ideas, patience, courage and good-humor. In a different way, for articulating what rare books "look like" to those who have never really looked, I am indebted to Melissa Garrity, Oscar Handlin, Lawrence P. Dowler, and Robert Alter; for photographing, not just the objects, but, miraculously, my idea of them, I thank Vic Santamaria, Dan Sullivan, and Rick Stafford. My colleagues Anne Anninger, Donald D. Eddy and Kenneth Lohf have graciously allowed me to exhibit items from the collections in their care. I have received material support from the Mellon Foundation, the Harvard Department of English and American Literature and Language, and the Harvard School of Continuing Education and University Extension; Mr. Arthur Rippey has generously contributed to the printing of the catalogue. I am very grateful to them all.

Above all, my catalogue is written in deep admiration

This Indenture ... made the third ... day of February in the eleventh year of the reign of our Sovereign Lord George the Second ... King of Great Britain ...

Between ...

Have ...

To have and to hold ...

To ...

To ...

To ...

To ...

To ...

To ...

And ...

And ...

In Witness whereof the parties first above named to these presents their hands and seals interchangeably have set their hands and seals the day and year first above written.

William ... Henry Fielding · Cath: Fielding · Ursula Fielding · Sarah Fielding · Beatrice Fielding · Edmund Fielding for a lawyer-collector whose first question, when I met him, was "What would you think if we sold the whole thing?" This was a poser, twenty years ago. But my greatest debt is to his wife, now Viscountess Eccles, who didn't sell the books, and indeed generously deposited them in Houghton for six long years, so that I could have something worth saying and an occasion for speaking. It is my tell, but her show: *Bibliotheca docet.*

HUGH AMORY

BIOGRAPHY ᢒᢒ

> He is a very indelicate, a very impetuous, an unyielding-spirited Man, and is capable of forming a Morality to his Practices.
>
> Samuel Richardson to Aaron Hill, 18 Aug. 1749.

> There was a great similitude between his character and that of Sir Richard Steele. He had the advantage both in Learning and, in my Opinion, Genius. They both agreed in wanting money in spite of all their Freinds, and would have wanted it if their Hereditary Lands had been as extensive as their Imagination, yet each of them so form'd for Happiness, it is pity they were not Immortal.
>
> Lady Mary Wortley Montagu to Lady Bute, 22 Sep. 1755.

Wall Case

1. Assignments of the Family Trust at East Stour, 3 Feb. 1737 [1738]. 62 × 73 cm.

Under a will of 1707, Fielding's grandfather, Sir Henry Gould, left £3,000 in trust for the separate use of his daughter, Sarah (1682–1718) and after her death to her issue—a common arrangement for the security of married women. On Sir Henry's death in 1710, his executors laid out the bequest in an estate at East Stour, Dorset worth £4,750, Fielding's father Edmund paying the balance. The part of the estate that they, Edmund and Sarah valued at £3,000 is particularly described in these documents as a farmhouse, yard, and outbuildings, with 185 acres of meadow and pasture called Breaches Close, Cleeves Field, Haverlands Close, Lawrence's Close, with "one close of meadow adjoyning", Broad Meads, Home Field, the Lady's Six Acres, North Field, Twelve Acres Field, Roe's Close, Press Closes, and "all those several closes adjoyning to the s^d messuage . . . known by the several names of Culver Hay, New Mead, and Milking Barton", together with right of pasturage for 32 beasts in East Stour Common.

In 1738, when the youngest child had reached his majority, the trustees under the will resigned their duties to the Gould family solicitor, Robert Stillingfleet; which required the two instruments shown here, in five large sheets of blue-stamped parchment, and the hands and seals of all six surviving children in order of seniority: Henry (1707–1754), Catharine (1708–1750), Ursula (1709–1750), Sarah (1710–1768), Beatrice (1714–1751) and Edmund (ba. 22 Apr. 1716).

Like many documents of Fielding's life, these (which turned up in a Bridgwater solicitor's office in 1911) have no archival or historical context. We know that a few months later Henry and his wife Charlotte seem to have sold an estate of 280 acres at East Stour for the ludicrous sum of £260. Cross, who misdated the assignments 1737, conjectured that they were preliminary to a partition of the trust; more likely, as Susan Staves suggests to me, the 1738 deed was part of a mortgage. In any case, Fielding (as usual) "wanted money."

Reference: CROSS (1918), p. 359–60

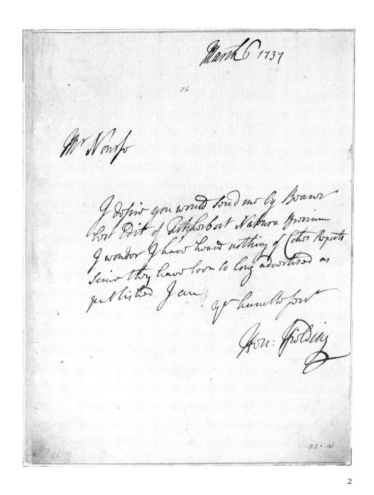

2

2. HF, Letter to John Nourse, 6 March 1737 [1738]. 19.5 × 15 cm.

One of four surviving letters from Fielding to this bookseller, one of the partners with Fielding and James Ralph in the *Champion,* 1739–1741. Together with a receipt for the translation of the *Military History of Charles XII* (1740), these documents evidently derive from an archive formerly in the possession of the nineteenth-century autograph collector, William Upcott; the bulk of the archive is now in the British Library (Add. MSS. 38,729). From Upcott, the letter passed successively to Dawson Turner (Puttick & Simpson, 6 June 1859, p. 275), John Young (Sotheby, 26 Apr. 1869, lot 347), "a foreign nobleman" (Sotheby, 17 Mar. 1875, lot 56), and the Drexel Institute, Philadelphia (Parke-Bernet, 17 Oct. 1944, lot 82) before the Hydes acquired it.

References: CROSS (1918), p. 360; TAYLOR (1960), no. 29; *Four Oaks* (1967), p. 35; FEATHER (1981)

3. HF, Letter to John Fielding, 12 July 1754.

One of five surviving letters (one fragmentary) written to his half-brother on a voyage to Lisbon for his health, where he died, 8 October 1754. These, and some letters to James "Hermes" Harris, are the only personal documents of his life.

Reference: AMORY, "Lisbon Letters" (1971)

4. TERENCE, Works. English & Latin / ed. Bernard. — Cantabrigiae, 1598.

One of four books known to survive from Fielding's library. The others are a Horace inscribed to Jane Collier, now in the University of California at Berkeley, James Drake's *Secret Memoirs of Leicester,* 2nd ed. (1706) in the University of Pennsylvania, and the remnants of Fielding's run of the *Covent-Garden Journal,* at the Bodleian. The Terence, which does not appear in the sale catalogue of Fielding's library, has no annotations, but is reliably certified by John Scott, who acquired it from Martha Fielding, the widow of Fielding's youngest son, William (d. 1820).

References: BAKER SALE (1755); Hall's Bookshop, Cat. 145 (1940), item 1; Anderson (H. Buxton Forman, pt. 2) 26 Apr. 1920, lot 1097; *Bibliotheca* (1983).

5. The Case of Marg^r Bell, 18 June [17]84.

Submitted for William Fielding's opinion as a barrister. No documents of Henry's professional practice survive (apart from formal records of appearances, signatures to motions, etc. which Ruthe Battestin has discovered), but this piece, by Henry's youngest son, gives a good idea of it. An early example of a barrister's opinion, which testifies to the still developing separation of the profession of a solicitor from that of a barrister.

Reference: AMORY (1968), no. 32 (misdated and wrongly ascribed to HF)

Digression: The Outside of a Text

The title of a book has moved from its fifteenth-century position at the back of the volume to successive layers in front: to the title-page (sixteenth century), half-title or added engraved t.-p. (seventeenth century), cover title (eighteenth century) and jacket title (nineteenth century). Only the fifteenth-century position recognizes the reality of production, that the preliminaries are ordinarily the last bit of text to be devised by the author and publisher. In this development, the publisher has gradually appropriated the intellectual property and an ever-increasing area of the market, until today his shadow falls even on the second-hand trade. Hence the significance of bindings for the history of publication: the original binding shows how the book became public; secondary bindings, how it was transferred to the private domain of a library — and ultimately, of course, back to where it belongs, in a human mind.

The crucial stage in this development is the publisher's appropriation of the binding. Most eighteenth-century London books were sold bound or in wrappers ("sewed"), but neither condition (when it survives) should be considered a "publisher's binding" 1) because the trade normally shared either the intellectual property or the sheets of most London books (cf. no. 8, below) and 2) because, before the introduction of printed wrappers and labels in the 1770's, there are no indicia of publication. Some original bindings may be considered "trade bindings", however: plain unlettered calf, as Graham Pollard suggests, or — a style introduced in the 1730's — half sheep and Dutch marbled boards. The second style is very common on books printed by Andrew Millar, Fielding's publisher after 1741, and since Millar presumably kept a stock of marbled paper to supply his binders, it is theoretically a "publisher's binding". Practically, however, we can hardly tell one stock of marbled paper from another.

References: POLLARD (1956); GASKELL (1972), p. 152

6. The late HF, Esq., *The Journal of a Voyage to Lisbon.* — London : A. Millar, 1755. The

edited, "Humphreys" version; second printed, first published.

————, *The Journal of a Voyage to Lisbon.* — London : A. Millar, 1755. The unedited, "Francis" version; first printed, second published.

These two versions, first identified by Austin Dobson in 1892, are conveniently distinguished by the name of Fielding's hosts at Ryde on the Isle of Wight: the Francises, as they actually were; or the Humphreys, as they fictionally became.

The establishment of the order of their printing and publication is one of the few triumphs of twentieth-century bibliography. Both are unmistakably fictionalized, and there can be no doubt that even the "unedited" version thoroughly distorts the day-to-day record that Fielding wrote. The Hyde Collection has four copies of the first edition: this copy is in its original trade binding of half sheep and marbled boards (cf. below, no. 69).

It has not been previously noted that, although William Strahan charged Millar for printing both editions, the ornaments are those of Samuel Richardson. Did Strahan farm the job out? Or is the criterion of ornaments, as some believe, unreliable?

Reference: CROSS (1918), p. 326

7. WILBUR L. CROSS, *The History of Henry Fielding.* — New Haven, 1918. 3 v.

Still the standard biography and bibliography — though the Wesleyan edition is gradually correcting the bibliography, and a new biography by Martin and Ruthe Battestin is eagerly awaited. This copy was annotated and

extra-illustrated by Cross's one competent rival—J. P. De Castro, a lawyer and antiquarian. The bittersweet pastime of tracking down Cross's errors and evasions—there is more or less one per page—consoled him for a lifetime of unpublished research, which Cross's biography preempted. The volumes later served in the reference department of the London bookseller, Francis Edwards.

Reference: Maggs, Cat. 1062 (1985)

CANON (SINCE CROSS)

There is not, I believe . . . a single Free Briton in this Kingdom, who hates his Wife more heartily than I detest the Muses. They have indeed behaved to me like the most infamous Harlots, and have laid many a spurious, as well as deformed Production at my Door.

Preface to *David Simple.* 2nd ed. (1744)

Wall Case

8. HF, Esq., *Works* / ed. Arthur Murphy. — London : Printed for W. Strahan, J. Rivington and Sons, {T. Payne}, S. Crowder, T. Longman, J. Robson, C. Dilly, G. Kearsly, G. Robinson, T. Cadell, T. Lowndes, R. Baldwin, {J. Nichols}, W. Cater, G. Nicoll, S. Bladon, J. Murray, W. Flexney, T. Evans, W. Otridge, J. Sewell, W. Lane, J. Bowen, & W. Fox, 1783. 12 v. Frontispiece (plate-mark): 15 × 8.8 cm.; with a photograph of a portrait of "Henry Fielding?" ascribed to Sir Joshua Reynolds (see frontispiece to this catalogue).

This selection, first published by Andrew Millar in 1762, eliminated most of Fielding's journalism in favor of literature. It set the canon for over a hundred years, and created the image of Fielding "the Novelist" under which he still appears in the *New Cambridge Bibliography of English Literature.*

The frontispiece, after William Hogarth, reenacts the rationale of the canon. The Sword of a gentleman and justice of peace, the Pen and Ink of a professional writer, and the Scales of Justice divide Fielding's "works" into two groups: legal achievements to his left, literary to his right. The Scales incline (naturally) to the Law. The prominent "Statutes at Large Vol. XIII" probably betoken the legislation for 13 George II (1740), when Fielding was called to the bar. Against it lean some cases presented for his legal opinion, one of which is unfolded (compare no. 5, above). The author's gaze, however, lingers on his novels, the latest of which is still open at the last page, as he left it. The laurels crowning the mask of Comedy (Tragedy is, literally, averted) confirm his true genius, in drama and romance; the suspiciously bushy eyebrows and long chin of Comedy seem to present a younger version of the portrait above, showing the author in the last months of his life. In brief, the frontispiece opposes the mute deeds of the Sword to the eloquent works of the Pen, the proper concern of this edition.

One reason that this canon persisted so long is that the property was widely shared in the London trade—some 24 partners appear in the 1783 imprint, in order of their seniority in the Stationers' Company (Thomas Payne was omitted by accident, and John Nichols appears only in the imprint of v. 2–12). All of their rights descend from the sale of Millar's property in 1769.

References: CROSS (1918), p. 328–9; PAULSON (1965), no. 248; BATTESTIN (1983); AMORY (1984)

MARY HAMILTON

J. Cruikshank fecit

The Prisoner being convicted of this base and scandalous crime was sentenced to be publicly and severely whipped four several times in 4 Market Towns, and to be imprisoned for 6 Months.   vide page 21.

9. [HF], *The Female Husband, or, The Surprising History of Mrs. Mary, alias Mr. George Hamilton.* — London, 1746.

A sensationalized account of a lesbian who was apprehended in Somerset and punished (on the advice of Fielding's cousin, Henry Gould) for "having by false and deceitful practices endeavoured to impose on some of his Majesty's subjects." Mary Hamilton's partners duly testified that they were quite unaware of her true sex.

Fielding's motives in writing are unclear: as always, he visibly delights in female grotesques; the testimony seemed to indicate a connection between Mary Hamilton's "unnatural" desires and Methodism, one of Fielding's *bêtes noires;* and he may have wished to publicize a defect in the law (female, as opposed to male, homosexual intercourse was not in itself criminal).

References: CROSS (1918), p. 313; BAKER (1959)

10. *The Female Husband, or, The Surprising History of Mrs. Mary, alias Mr. George Hamilton.* — London : M. Jones, [ca. 1750?]. 8vo: [−]⁴; 7, [1] p.

An unrecorded chapbook version, which reduces the subject to its most banal — women in drag; the very stuff of romance, as Shakespeare's comedies testify. The printer is unidentified and may be pseudonymous or provincial (Shrewsbury?).

11. *The Surprising Adventures of a Female Husband!* — London, [1813]. Frontispiece: 18 × 21 cm.

Another chapbook version, this one inclining to salacity; with a vivid frontispiece by George Cruikshank.

References: GREEN (1902), II, 464; COHN (1924), no. 314

12. *An Attempt towards a Natural History of the Hanover Rat.* — London, 1744.

Uncut copy.
This amusing spoof on the Royal Society shows a preference for third-person verb-forms in *th*, including Fielding's characteristic "hath" and "doth"; on which basis it has been ascribed to him. The anti-Hanoverian bias, though it may surprise those who are acquainted with Squire Western, is Fielding's normal political stance before the Jacobite Rebellion. Though the *New Cambridge Bibliography of English Literature* accepts the attribution, more recent work rejects the criterion.

References: JENSEN (1935); BATTESTINS (1980)

13. "JAMES MACPHERSON" [HF], *The History of the Present Rebellion in Scotland.* — London, 1745.

Cross, who never saw a copy, made a thorough muddle of identifying it, confusing it with *A Compleat History of the Rebellion* (1747), which is not by Fielding (also in the Hyde Collection). This is the only work of Fielding that was reprinted in America during his lifetime.

References: CROSS (1918), p. 310; JARVIS (1945); Parke-Bernet (Herbert L. Carlebach) 20 Jan. 1948, lot 55 (this copy)

14. [HF], *The Charge to the Jury, or, The Sum of the Evidence on the Trial of A.B.C.D. and E.F., all M.D.* — London, 1745.

225

The only known uncut copy.

A satire on the physicians attending the deathbed of Sir Robert Walpole (now Earl of Orford), and a defense of Fielding's surgeon-friend, John Ranby. Here as elsewhere, Fielding sides with practical medicine against the learned tradition of the universities; with surgeons like Ranby and "quacks" like "Spot" Ward against physicians and their allies the apothecaries.

References: CROSS (1918), p. 338 (conjecturally dated 1748?); JARVIS (1946)

15. "Captain COCKADE" [TIMOTHY BRECK-NOCK], *The Important Triflers.* — London, 1748.

One of eleven known copies of this satire on the foibles of fashionable women; ascribed to Fielding in a Dublin reprint (followed by Cross). A MS ascription to Brecknock in a copy of the original at L is far more credible.

References: CROSS (1918), p. 316; FOXON B405

16. [HF], *Some Thoughts on the Present State of the Theatres, and the Consequences of an Act to destroy the Liberty of the Stage.* — [London, 1737]. fol.: [–]²; 3, [1] p. (filing title on p. [4]).

The unique surviving copy of this pamphlet; a reprinting appeared in the *Daily Journal*, 25 Mar. 1737.

References: ARNOTT 171; LOCKWOOD (1980); LIESENFELD (1984) p. 221, n. 43

> O, *Shakespear*, had I thy Pen! O, *Hogarth*, had I thy Pencil!
>
> *Tom Jones*, X.8.

Wall Case

17. [PIERRE SIMON, *The Philosopher Square discover'd by Tom Jones.* — London, 1787?]. 34.7 × 44.2 cm.

Engraved after the painting by John Downman exhibited at the Royal Academy; proof, before lettering, with the figures of Square and Molly incompletely finished. The location of the original is unknown, but a studio copy (?) was recently offered at Sotheby's (color photograph).

The illustration has an air of the stage (note how the "actors" take account of an "audience"), but no dramatic version of *Tom Jones* contained this scene, which indeed was too "low" for dramatic representation. It belongs to the vogue for "historical paintings" whose crown is Boydell's Shakespeare (1782–1802).

Reference: Sotheby (anon.) 16 Nov. 1983, lot 92

Floor Case

18. "SCRIBLERUS Secundus" [HF], *Tom Thumb.* — London [i.e. The Hague?], 1730. 12mo: π1, A–B⁶; [8], 18 p.

An unrecorded reprint, on French paper. The passage of the Copyright Act of 1710 allowed the London trade to brand as "piracies" an ever-growing volume of Scottish, Irish and Continental reprints, most of them legal except for sale in England and Scotland. They were presumably pirated because the London trade was incapable of supplying provincial demand.

How much of the *London* market these "piracies" actually stole is a harder question; but it should be noted that the provincial printers had the same problem of distribution as the London trade, and far less capital.

Reference: ELIAS (1984)

19. "H. SCRIBLERUS Secundus" [HF], *The Tragedy of Tragedies.* — London, 1731. Frontispiece (platemark): 18.1 × 10.8 cm.

Illustrations provided a literary property with a trademark that a provincial printer usually could not copy: not only did a plate cost nearly as much as the letterpress of a play or pamphlet, but the technology of engraving was not generally available outside London. In this case, spurred on by the Hague *Tom Thumb,* John Watts not only secured a frontispiece from William Hogarth, but a revised text and title from Fielding.

Not surprisingly, the illustrative value of such "trademarks" is often low. Hogarth is an exception — and not only in portraying the dramatic fiction, instead of picturing, as usual, the performance:

GLUMDALCA
I need not ask if you are *Huncamunca,*
Your Brandy Nose proclaims———
HUNCAMUNCA
I am a Princess;
Nor need I ask who you are.
GLUMDALCA
A Giantess . . . (Act II, Scene 2)

Tom is dressed as a Knight of the Garter.

References: CROSS (1918), p. 292; PAULSON (1965), no. 220

20. HF, Esq., *The History of the Adventures of Joseph Andrews.* — 3rd ed. — London, 1743. 2 v.

The first illustrated edition, and the first to name the author.

The illustrations and the statement of authorship respond to a piracy of which no copy survives; we know of it only through lawsuits — *Millar* v. *Lynch* (1742), charging that Daniel and Ann Lynch (otherwise unknown) sold such a piracy in London (P.R.O., C. 41/5, no. 66); and *Midwinter* et al. v. *Hamilton* et al. (1744 – 1750), where the defendants alleged that "the Adventures of Joseph Andrews were pirated at London, and sent to Edinburgh by Mr. Hodges . . . who now pursues [i.e. prosecutes] the retalers for selling a book . . . pirated by himself" — EN: Advocates Library, Arniston Coll., v. 20 (1745 – 48), case 32, no. 9 (29 June 1747).

Reference: CROSS (1918), p. 306 (omits statement of authorship)

21. HF, Esq., *The History of Tom Jones, a Foundling.* — Dublin : J. Smith, 1749. 3 v.

First Irish edition, printed from advance sheets provided by the London publisher.

Like Western publishers in Taiwan today, London booksellers occasionally tried to cut their losses by helping one "pirate" to scoop the rest (presumably, for a fee). This Dublin reprint must have been set from advance sheets because it has corrected leaves (cancels) reprinted at the same points in v. 1 – 2 as the London edition — text that was only supplied with the last volume of the London edition. John and his partner William Smith so often appear as reprinters of Millar's books that we must

W. Hogarth inv:.   Ger VanderGucht sculp.

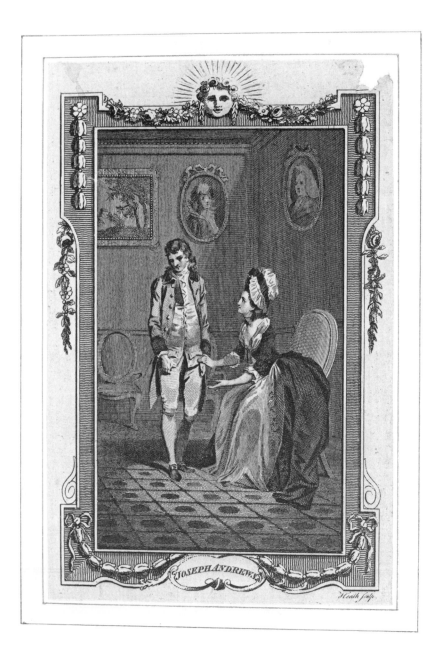

JOSEPH ANDREWS

Heath sculp.

infer a standing arrangement. Such editions might usefully be distinguished as "sanctioned reprints". Parallels are known for American reprints of Scott's novels.

References: RANDALL (1935); PHILLIPS (1952); AMORY (1977); NERBONNE (1978)

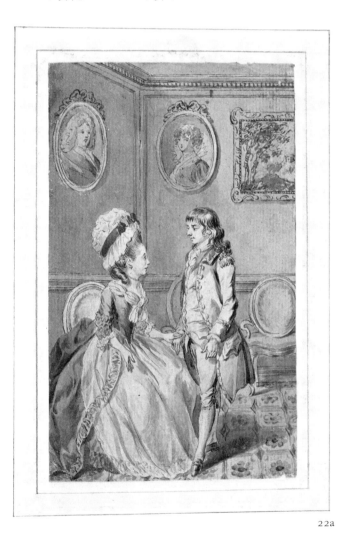

22a

22. [THOMAS STOTHARD], Ink and wash drawing for *Joseph Andrews*, with an india-paper proof of James Heath's engraving after it for James Harrison's *Novelists Magazine*, v. 3 (1781). 2 p. (frame): 13 × 8.3 cm.; 16.2 × 10.9 cm.

The defeat of the London trade's claim to perpetual literary property in 1774 led to an explosion of reprints of the previously protected properties, all in series: Bell's British Theatre, Harrison's Novelists Magazine, and Cooke's Select British Novels are the best known. They are the major market and school for English engravers in the second half of the century. The need for editorial control in a series, and the publishers' endeavour to make these old warhorses "new" seems to have introduced a much greater degree of "illustrativeness".

In this example, the publisher (or perhaps the engraver) has brought Stothard's drawing much closer to the text: Lady Booby changes from a flirtatious *demimondaine* to an imperious society dame; Joseph has grown from a somewhat knowing (though very surprised) Ganymede to a bashful Apollo. It is a worse drawing — wholly devoid of sexual tension — but a better illustration.

23. [HF], *The Mock Doctor, or, The Dumb Lady Cur'd* / from Molière. — 2nd ed. — London : J. Wells, 1735. small (foolscap) 8vo: A–D⁴; iv, {5}–32 p.

Unrecorded piracy, with parodic imprint; disbound, probably from a duodecimo tract volume.

One of the curious features of English piracies is their tendency to parody the names of the genuine printers and

Moreau j inv   mariage aquâ forti.

24a

publishers: "J. Wells" substitutes for "J. Watts," "C. Borbet" for "C. Corbett", "T. Doddesley" for "J. Dodsley", etc. Like lowcut dresses, which reveal as well as conceal, the practice seems to have a moral origin. Irish reprints rarely conceal their origin, probably because so few were actually sold in England.

24. L. F. MARIAGE, "voisin, si vous ne m'en croyez pas, vous pouvez le lui demander vous-même", in v. 4 of *Tom Jones*. — Paris, 1833; from a suite of 12 engravings by Mariage and others after Moreau le jeune: a) Large paper, before lettering [Paris, 1816?] 12.6 × 8.2 cm. (image); b) Ordinary paper, hand-colored and inlaid as an extra-illustration in v. 3 of *The History of Tom Jones, a Foundling*. — Edinburgh, 1791.

Engraved in 1816, shortly after Moreau's death, and probably published separately before lettering; the plates were later cut down from an average of 24.5 × 16.5 cm. to 16.5 × 9 cm. for issue in the Comte de La Bédoyère's translation of *Tom Jones* (1833), on three grades of paper, including *papier de chine* (a set of which is also bound into this extra-illustrated copy). These transformations underline the prestige of Parisian engraving, which could command a market independently of its illustrative function.

Reference: BOCHER (1882), no. 544 (1st & 3rd states)

25. HF, Esquire, *The History of Tom Jones, a Foundling*. — New York, [1795]. (Robertson and Gowan's Select Novels)   3 v.

The first illustrated American edition (the first American edition appeared only a year earlier).

By 1795, Charles Cooke's Select British Novels had captured the classic novel market from the London trade — incidentally defining the canon of the eighteenth-century novel in the process. Not only did he kill off the editions of the proprietors, but also the Scottish and Irish "piracies". Counterfeit reprints of his series in Ireland and America testify to his success.

Five other copies (N, MWA, MSaE, VaU; L (uncat.)) of this American counterfeit are known, every one of which contains a different mixture of sheets, printed 1795 – ca. 1810. The six copies represent two imprints (the other, New York: Benjamin Gomez, [1797?]) in five distinct issues, including one in England without the plates; and they testify to a sixth, Philadelphia issue in numbers, of which no copy survives. The study of such evidence for the distribution of books in America is still in its fetal state.

References: Stuart Bennett, Cat. 5 (1983), item 73 (= L); GILREATH (1986); not in EVANS

GRUBSTREET LETTERS

For my own Part, I never walk into Mrs. Dodd's Shop, and survey all that vast and formidable Host of Papers and Pamphlets arranged on her Shelves, but the noble Lamentation of Xerxes occurs to my Mind; who, when he reviewed his Army, on the Banks of the Hellespont, is said to have grieved, for that not one of all those Hundreds of Thousands would be living an Hundred Years from that Time.

Covent-Garden Journal, no. 6

Fielding conducted five — possibly six — periodicals: in Opposition, *The Champion,* 1739 – 41, and perhaps, as Martin Battestin proposes, a large part of *The Craftsman,* 1734 – 38; for the Ministry, *The True Patriot* (1745 – 46) and *The Jacobite's Journal* (1747 – 48); without any clear political affiliation, a fortnightly magazine, *The History of Our Own Times* (1741); and *The Covent-Garden Journal* (1752). Journalism and the Bar were his main livelihood between his abandonment of the stage in 1737 and his appointment as justice of the peace for Westminster, ten years later.

The advent of printing threw English orthography into confusion, from which it did not recover in print before 1650, or in manuscript before 1700. Journalism, rather than *belles-lettres,* was probably the forum where these conventions were hammered out, and the public, not printers, authors, or spelling-reformers, were the arbiters. Fielding was one of the first to exploit the new conventions for satire, lashing the following "illiterates": people of the past or of the future, working-class figures with any hope of leisure (including criminals), would-be *robins* (attorney's clerks and country J.P.'s), beaux (i.e. effeminate high society), and women. This extraordinary collection of "outsiders" implicitly defines what Fielding saw as his public — the broad masses of educated, male, eighteenth-century English gentry. Small wonder that literacy stagnated during the eighteenth century.

References: SCRAGG (1974); CRESSY (1980), p. 177; SPUFFORD (1981), p. 62f.; LOCKWOOD (1986); BATTESTIN (1986)

26. *The Jacobite's Journal : no. 3* (19 Dec. 1747) / ed. "John Trott-plaid, Esq." [HF]. — London : Sold by M. Cooper, C. Corbett, and G. Woodfall, 1747. Detail: 26 × 20 cm.

THE
JACOBITE's JOURNAL.

By JOHN TROTT-PLAID, *Esq*;

SATURDAY, DECEMBER 19, 1747.   NUMB. 3.

An unrecorded issue, with variant imprint: all other surviving copies were "Sold by M. Cooper, G. Woodfall, C. Corbett & Mrs. Nutt." Elizabeth Nutt, like Ann Dodd, was a "mercury woman" or jobber, who supplied the newspapers and pamphlets sold by hawkers to the public. They are occasionally named in imprints. The format is typical of weekly periodicals in the first half of the century: 4 p., in 2 columns small pica per page; containing a lead essay ("leader"), news and advertisements (2/ each, one-half for the government).

The woodcut (dubiously ascribed to Hogarth) shows the editor and his termagant wife Peggy in Scotch plaids, both drunk from treasonable toasts. A hypocritical friar draws their ass with the bait, so to speak, of an Opposition newspaper; while a copy of Harrington's *Oceana* bound in the Lilies of France spurs it on behind. The whole was meant as an emblem of "that notable and mysterious union of French Interest, Popery, Jacobitism and Republicanism" (*JJ*, no. 13), but the burlesque was apparently misunderstood and Fielding dropped the illustration in that issue and eventually abandoned his Jacobite pose in no. 17. His irony was most successful when he was pretending to be himself; polar reversals like Trottplaid or the author-editor of *Jonathan Wild* got out of hand.

References: Sotheby (Rev. Henry Wellesley, ex Horace Walpole) 8 Nov. 1866, lot 4195; CROSS (1918), p. 315–16; Birrell & Garnett, Cat. 26 [1930], no. 55; Blackwell's, Cat. A2 (1979–80), no. 33; P. M. Hill, Cat. 159 (1982), no. 9; WESLEYAN ED. (1975)

27. *The Champion* / ed. "Capt. Hercules Vinegar" [HF and James Ralph]. — London,

1741. 2 v.; with the bookplate of John, Lord Somers (son of the great politician).

A reprint of the leaders for 15 Nov. 1739 to 19 June 1740. Collections of leaders have served to represent periodicals since the *Tatler* and *Spectator*. A comparison of these neat volumes with the rugged mass of the *Covent-Garden Journal*'s original numbers shows how much is lost: here are pages, pretending to be columns.

Fielding apparently stopped contributing to the *Champion* by February 1741 (the evidence is conflicting). The extant runs of the original numbers are defective before 29 Dec. 1739 and after 15 Nov. 1740, and must still be supplemented by this somewhat unreliable collection and reprinted leaders or extracts elsewhere.

References: CROSS (1918), p. 304–5; P. M. Hill, Cat. 58 (1957), no. 25; CLEARY (1984), p. 117f.; LOCKWOOD (1986)

28. *The Covent-Garden Journal* / ed. "Sir Alexander Drawcansir" [HF]. — London, 1752. Nos. 1–12, 14–70, 72.

A nearly complete run of the original numbers; seven other comparable sets survive, the most for any periodical of Fielding's (CtY, TxU; L, O (HF's copy), LU; Sotheby (Rev. Henry Wellesley, ex Horace Walpole) 8 Nov. 1866, lot 4195; W. H. Robinson, Cat. 63 (1937), no. 73A).

In a convention dating from ca. 1750, we capitalize the first letters of proper names and lowercase most other nouns; before 1750 and in most of Fielding's published work, most nouns had initial capitals, as in German (nouns in adverbial and prepositional phrases are frequent exceptions), and proper names were distinguished by italics. The rough equivalent of our emphatic italics was SMALL CAPITALS. Uniquely of the works of Fielding that he saw in print, the *Covent-Garden Journal* preserves the capitalization and italicization found in his literary manuscripts. This must be Fielding's deliberate choice — the equivalent, under our present-day convention, of writing all proper names with small initial letters. The punctuation of Fielding's manuscripts, however, is normally much lighter than that of his printed works.

References: CROSS (1918), p. 362–3; Chas. J. Sawyer, Cat. 190 (1948), no. 238 (this copy); HONAN (1960); OSSELTON (1985)

29a. JONATHAN RICHARDSON, Sr., *Explanatory Notes* and *Remarks on Milton's* Paradise Lost. — London, 1734.
b. EDWARD YOUNG, *Love of Fame, the Universal Passion.* — 2nd ed. — London, 1728.
2 p.: 20.5 × 13 cm.; 19 × 15 cm.

The new standard of orthography was far from rigid at first: we find many minor variants, such as *critic/critick/critique*. Nevertheless, it was sufficiently uniform to give personal choice (or by-gone choice) a new expressiveness. Richardson uppercases for emphasis, leaving even the unemphatic beginnings of sentences in lower case. Young achieves the same effect by emphatic italics. It is but a step to the forgeries of George Steevens and Thomas Chatterton, who supposed that "old-spelling" was a guarantee of historical authenticity. Orthography, which was only *ad hoc* or "occasional" in the earlier periods, has become a rhetorical device.

References: BRONSON (1958); FOXON, *Lyell Lectures* (1975)

GRUBSTREET LAW ૭

The gentlemen of the Western Circuit have a tradition concerning Fielding, which, though somewhat inconsistent with the account that Mr. Murphy has given of him, yet is perfectly agreeable to the idea generally entertained of his humour and character. Having attended the judges two or three years without the least prospect of success, he published proposals for a new law-book; which being circulated round the country, the young barrister was, at the ensuing assizes, loaded with briefs at every town on the circuit. But his practice thus suddenly increased, almost as suddenly declined.

The London Chronicle (Apr. 1762), 324n.

The legal profession in England has always been relatively small compared to that of the United States — about 150 persons at the bar in Fielding's day, when a single serjeant might monopolize the entire practice of a circuit. The solicitors had only begun to organize their profession, and as "attorneys" were still generally considered a litigious, low-class lot of "caterpillars". Barristers, then as now, were the "distinguished" branch of the profession — now led by a new rank, King's Counsel; the older leaders, Serjeants, were already figures of fun.

Fielding was well-connected for a legal career; his grandfather had been a judge of King's Bench, and his uncle was a Bencher of the Middle Temple. Nevertheless he faced an uncertain financial future when he was called to the bar of the Middle Temple in 1740. Most of his earnings at first probably derived from drafting "special pleas" or running errands for his uncle, as an attorney, to which he later added the office of J.P. At all times, he used his position as a barrister to authenticate his journalism. Today, any one of these practices would be grounds for disbarment. Fielding's rhetoric continues to sway modern critics, who read his productions as "social and legal pamphlets", as though they enjoyed some professional privilege.

30. [HF], "An Institute of the Pleas of the Crown", MS, ca. 1745.

This two-volume work by Fielding survives only in fragments, which his grandson W. H. Fielding dispersed on the nineteenth-century autograph market. The table of contents and a leaf from the chapter on Petit Treason are at Harvard; the largest fragment (and Fielding's largest surviving manuscript), a chapter on Outlawry, is in the Hyde Collection; and two leaves from chapters on Public Felonies and Respiting Judgment are at Yale, the last of which shows that Fielding never finished the treatise. Note the display hand of the title, which Fielding occasionally uses within the text for emphasis. An edition has been published as a keepsake of this exhibition.

Reference: AMORY (1968)

31. HF, Esq., Barrister at Law, and one of His Majesty's Justices of the Peace for the County of Middlesex, and for the City and Liberty of Westminster, *A True State of the Case of Bosavern Penlez.* — London, 1749.

Penlez, the barber son of a West-country clergyman, was arrested during some riotous assaults on bawdy houses in Bloomsbury, mostly by gangs of sailors who claimed that one of their number had been bilked by the proprietor. Fielding was in the awkward position, as committing magistrate, of defending law and order for neighborhood pimps and whores whom it was his legal duty to suppress. He also owed his office of J.P. (and other favors) to the Duke of Bedford, the largest property-owner in the area, and duly reported all his measures against the rioters to him. This was in no way illegal, but the public all too readily perceived that Fielding was in Bedford's "pocket." The death penalty imposed by the Riot Act was harsh, there were "constitutional" doubts about its restrictions on freedom of assembly, and the jury had recommended Penlez to mercy. Worse, in the aftermath of Penlez' execution, Lord Trentham, Bedford's son-in-law, ran in a Westminster bye-election, and the popular outcry threatened his chances.

In this rather unlikeable pamphlet, Fielding donned his barrister's robes and argued that the only issues were legal: that Penlez was justly condemned for rioting; but that even if he had been acquitted of that charge, he would in any case have been hanged for looting. Bringing an unproven crime to the attention of the authorities in order to defeat a plea for mercy is cruel; bringing it to the attention of the public after the man is hanged is either pointless or self-interested.

References: CROSS (1918), p. 319–20; LINEBAUGH (1975); BATTESTINS (1978); LANGBEIN, "Fatal Flaws" (1983)

32. "A Gentleman not Concern'd" [JOHN CLELAND], *The Case of the Unfortunate Bosavern Penlez.* — 2nd ed. — London, 1750 [1749].

The authorship of this pamphlet, by Fielding's fellow novelist, has only recently come to light. Cleland's only reply to Fielding's legalism was to reissue his anonymous defense of Penlez with a cancel t.-p. and half-title, describing himself, pointedly, as "a gentleman not concern'd."

Reference: LONSDALE (1979)

what is done very Commonly, That of re-
quiring a Child to read what He or She as
little Underſtands, or takes Pleaſure in as
theſe Girls did his Latin, Greek, Hebrew, &c?
'tis true, they were kept from what was More
Delightful. and Happy would it be were
Young People kept, even Thus, from What
Moſt Nowadays are Educated in; Happy
to Themſelves, as well as to Thoſe who
in Reality Love them Beſt; and That, not
Only for the Preſent, but Throughout every
Stage of their Future Life.

but Admitting it was a Hardſhip; let the Father be taken into the Account, let Some regard
be had to Him. Here was an Old Man, Blind,
Infirm, near Ruin'd, Afflicted; Standing in
greatNeed therefore ofAſſiſtance fromThoſe of
Whom he had reaſon to Expect it, and of what
Conſolation They could Afford; One of the
Principal Branches of which was Reading, and
Writing for him. he was not in a Condition
to Hire a Proper Perſon Always to Attend as
his Own Children, or, if he would have done
That, he muſt have Leſſen'd his Proviſion for
his Family. They were Then at Work for
Themſelves. and was it Nothing (think ye)
no Hardſhip upon Him to Teach Girls as
Theſe were Taught? Conſider His Diſtreſs,
Either way; and Pity Him you have been
Blaming, and Who was by Much the Greater
Sufferer, whether They Aſſiſted Him or did
not; and Conſider Withall that They Deſerv'd

b 3   the

I find the *fool*, when I behold the *skreen*;
For 'tis the wife man's intereft to be *fecn*.

   Hence, ———, that opennefs of heart,
And juft difdain for that poor *mimic*, Art;
Hence (manly praife!) that manner nobly free,
Which all admire, and I commend in thee.

   With generous fcorn how oft haft thou furvey'd
Of *court*, and *town* the noon-tyde Mafquerade,
Where fwarms of *knaves* the Vizor quite difgrace,
And hide fecure behind a *naked face?*
Where nature's end of language is declin'd,
And men talk only to *conceal* the mind;
Where generous hearts the greateft hazard run,
And he who trufts a *brother* is undone?

   Thefe all their care expend on outward fhow
For Wealth, and Fame; for Fame alone, the *Beau.*

33. HF, Esq., Barrister at Law and one of His Majesty's Justices of the Peace for the County of Middlesex, and for the City and Liberty of Westminster, *An Enquiry into the Causes of the Late Increase of Robbers.* — London, 1751.

Uncut copy, in original blue-gray wrappers.

The moral responsibility of the crime wave, in Fielding's view, belonged to the rich, whose "luxury" placed irresistible temptations in the path of the poor. He proposed to balance the books on the debit side, by imposing severer penalties for theft, by increasing the incentives for prosecution, and by making it more difficult to dispose of stolen goods. The interest of these views lies less in their originality than in their universal acceptance. One of the few to dissent was Dr. Johnson in *Rambler* no. 114, published a few months later and almost certainly a criticism of Fielding.

Since Fielding's views were commonplace, it is hard to say whether they had any specific effect or not. An act of 1752, adding the terrors of dissection to those of death for murder; and a bill of 1752, regulating pawnbrokers, have been claimed for his influence.

References: CROSS (1918), p. 320–21; Parke-Bernet (Herbert L. Carlebach) 20 Jan. 1948, lot 52; ZIRKER (1966); AMORY, "Criminal Legislation" (1971); LANGBEIN, "Trial" (1983)

34. THE PROPRIETORS [HF, John Fielding, Saunders Welch, and others], *A Plan of the Universal Register-Office opposite Cecil-Street . . . and of that in Bishopsgate-Street.* — London, 1752.

An uncut copy of the second edition; only three copies of the first (1751, not in Cross: CSmH, CtY; L) are known.

Fielding's most innovative scheme for reforming society, a combination lost-and-found, employment, booking, and real estate office, which his blind half-brother John operated. To prove its utility, Fielding introduced the office (anachronistically) into his novel *Amelia.*

References: CROSS (1918), p. 321; GEORGE (1929)

35. *Examples of the Interposition of Providence in the Detection and Punishment of Murder* / collected from various authors, antient and modern, with an introduction and conclusion, both written by Henry Fielding, Esq;. — London, 1752. ⟨Price bound one shilling, or ten shillings a dozen to those who give them away.⟩

Original sheep (the cheapest binding), rebacked.

This tiny book, distilled from the massive folios (in xerox) of John Reynolds, *The Triumphs of God's Revenge against Murder* (1635), Nathaniel Wanley's *Wonders of the Little World* (1678), and William Turner's *Compleat History of the Most Remarkable Providences . . . in the Present Age* (1697), is a more practical response to the crime wave than Fielding's *Enquiry.* Cross gratuitously ascribed the compilation to Sarah Fielding or William Young, yet Fielding naturally assumed the pose of an editor in order to present these oppressive and lackluster fables as sober fact.

And what an unexpected piece of work it is from the creator of *Tom Jones!* yet it enjoyed a European reputation, with translations into French, German, Dutch and

Danish. Fielding's only experiment in working-class literature, it was designed to be "given away" — by masters, no doubt, to servants, but also by parents to children and even by regimental commanders to their troops, as the *Covent-Garden Journal* reported. Hannah More reprinted Fielding's pioneering pre-Victorian tract in her Cheap Repository series (1793).

Reference: CROSS (1918), p. 324

DRAMA ༄

> While Hisses, Groans, and Cat-calls thro' the Pit,
> Deplore the hapless Poet's want of Wit:
> *J(oh)n W(at)ts,* from Silence bursting in a Rage,
> Cry'd, *Men are mad who write in such an Age.*
> *Not so,* reply'd his Friend, a sneering Blade,
> *The Poet's only dull, the Printer's mad.*
>
> *Miscellanies,* v. 1.

36. HF, Esq., *The Dramatick Works.* — London : J. Watts, [1742?]. 2 v.

The first collection of Fielding's works, generally dated 1745 in modern reference sources, but already an object of satire by 1740; it is a reissue of Watts's nineteen separately published properties with general title-pages (probably printed ca. 1741) directing the binder how to make them up into volumes. Such "nonce collections", as they are called, are typical of sermons, plays, and poetry, all of which were printed in uniform formats for this eventuality.

The contents of earlier issues of the collected plays, without general t.-p.'s, are very similar: taking the order

assigned on the general t.-p.'s, v. 1 of the Folger copy contains I.1,2,3,4,5,6,7,8, II.9, I.9; and the Stockhausen copy (Sotheby-Parke Bernet, 19 Nov. 1974, lot 186) contains I.1,2,3,4,5,6,7,8,9, and II.2,1,4,5,3, 8,7,10,6,9. In contemporary bindings, they are almost certainly "as published", not copies that have lost their general t.-p.'s. Watts presumably had no motive for issuing the collection before 1737, when Fielding quit the stage.

References: [HF], *The Tryal of Colley Cibber, Comedian, &c.* (London, 1740), p. 40; CROSS (1918), p. 311–12

37. HF, Esq., *The Dramatic Works.* — London : A. Millar, 1755 [i.e. 1756?]. 3 v.

Millar bought Watts's stock, added a previously published property of his own, *Miss Lucy in Town* (1742), and reprinted the suppressed *Grub-Street Opera* and *The Masquerade* (1728) to fill out the collection. The inclusion of *The Masquerade,* a poem, and the exclusion of *The Wedding-Day,* a drama reprinted in the *Miscellanies,* suggest that Millar eventually projected an even larger nonce collection, of Fielding's octavos. Like Watts, Millar continued to print new editions as stock ran short; this collection was still on sale in 1775 by Millar's successors. For a conspectus of the seventeen known complete copies, representing seven distinct issues, see diagram, p. 30–31.

References: AMORY, "First Recension" (1981)

38. "SCRIBLERUS Secundus" [HF], *The Grub-Street Opera . . . ; to which is added, The Masquerade, a Poem.* — London : J. Roberts, 1731 [i.e. A. Millar, 1755].

FIELDING'S DRAMATIC WORKS 1737?–1765

	ROBERTS FOR WATTS			WATTS			MILLAR
	f. J. Roberts	pr. & sold by J. Roberts	f. J. Watts & sold by J. Roberts	f. J. Watts	by & f. J. Watts; sold by him & W. Reeve	by & f. J. Watts	f. A. Millar
Love in sev'l masques				1728 ▼●○○■·□			
Temple beau	1730			1730 ▼●○○■·□			
Author's farce	1730 1730			2d ed., 1730 ▼●○ 3d ed., 1750 ■·□			
Coffee-house politician¹				1730 ▼●○○■·□			
Tragedy of tragedies²		1731		3d ed., 1737 ▼●○○		4th ed., 1751 ■·□	1765
Letter-writers		1731 ▼●○○		1750 ■·□			
Lottery				1732 2d ed., 1732 3d ed., 1732 ▼●○ 4th ed., 1748 ○■·			
Modern husband				1732 ▼●○○ 2d ed., 1732 ■·□			
(Old) debauchees			1732 ▼●		2d ed., 1746 [1745] ●		5th ed., 1761 □
Covent-Garden tragedy			1732 ▼●○○	1754 ■·□		3d ed., 1750 ○■·□	

Mock doctor	2d ed., 1732 ▼ · 3d ed., 1742 ●◉○ · 4th ed., 1753 ■▪ · new ed., 1761 □
Miser	1733 ●▼ · 2d ed., 1744 ◉○ · 3d ed., 1754 ■▪ · 4th ed., 1761 □
Intriguing chambermaid	1734 ●●○ · 1750 ■▪ · new ed., 1761 □
Don Quixote in England	1734 ●●○ · 1754 ■▪ □
Old man taught wisdom	1735 · 2d ed., 1735 ▼ · 3d ed., 1742 ●◉ · 4th ed., 1749 ○■▪ □
Universal gallant	1735 ●▼○○ ■ □
Pasquin	1736 ▼ · 2d ed., 1740 ●◉○ · 3d ed., 1754 ■▪ □
Tumbledown Dick	1736 ●▼ · 1744 ◉○ ■ □
Historical register	[1737]⁴ ▼ · 1741 ●◉○ ■▪
Miss Lucy in town	1742 ■ · 2d ed., 1756 ■▪
Grubstreet opera	"f. J. Roberts, 1731" ■ · [1755] ■▪□

Issues

- ▼ [1737?] STOCKHAUSEN (gen. t.-p.'s absent)
- ● [1742?] DFo (gen. t.-p. absent in v. 1), NIC
- ◉ [1746?] CtY
- ○ [1750?] DLC
- ■ 1755 InU, MH NN (Berg), NIC, PU; O
- ▪ 1755 [i.e. 1756?] HYDE, PPRF
- □ 1755 [i.e. 1761?] CtY(2), CSmH, NNC

Notes

1. A reissue with cancel t.-p. of *Rape upon rape.*
2. A revised version of *Tom Thumb* (1730)
3. Also reissued with cancel prelims. "by & f. J. Watts; sold by him & W. Reeve, 1746 [1745]."
4. Also reissued with cancel t.-p. "f. W. Bickerton, 1744."

PASQUIN.

ACT I. SCENE I.

SCENE, *The Play-House.*

Enter several Players.

1st PLAYER.

HEN does the Rehearsal begin?
2d *Player.* I suppose we shall
hardly Rehearse the Comedy this
Morning ; for the Author was Arrested as he was going home from
King's Coffee-house ; and as I
heard, it was for upwards of Four
Pound : I suppose he will hardly get Bail.

1st *Player.* Where's the Tragedy-Author then? I
have a long Part in both, and it's past Ten o'Clock:

Wom. *Player.* Ay, I have a Part in booth too ; I
wish any one else had them, for they are not seven
Lengths put together. I think it is very hard a Woman, of my Standing, should have a short Part put
upon her. I suppose Mrs. *Merit* will have all our
principal Parts now, but I'm resolv'd I'll Advertise a-
gainst her : I'll let the Town know how I am in-
jured.

1st *Player.* Oh ! here comes our Tragedy-Poet.
Enter

Apparently a reprint of a lost, genuine edition that Fielding had suppressed. James Roberts (d. 1754) was a "trade publisher", who specialized in distributing other people's properties under his own name: such a service was particularly convenient for politically sensitive or privately printed material.

The reprint has proved deceptive, because Millar's collection was often "disbound" (like this copy) for separate sale in the nineteenth and twentieth centuries. The false imprint was presumably an attempt at uniformity with the Roberts imprints of other plays in the collection, not an effort to deceive. Since the collection was posthumous, there is some question of Millar's authority for printing it: Fielding had reused some of the songs in *The Lottery* (1732), *Don Quixote in England* (1734), and elsewhere.

References: CROSS (1918), p. 293; MORISSEY (1973); TREAD-WELL (1982)

39. "SCRIBLERUS Secundus" [HF], *The Welsh Opera, or, The Grey Mare the Better Horse.* — London : Printed for E. Rayner, and sold by the booksellers of London and Westminster, 1731.

An early version of *The Grub-Street Opera;* this edition is a "bad octavo", i.e. an unauthorized, memorially reconstructed version, printed by a notorious London pirate.

Reference: CROSS (1918), p. 293 (variant imprint)

40. "SCRIBLERUS Secundus" [HF], *The Genuine Grub-Street Opera*. London : For the benefit of the comedians [i.e. E. Rayner], 1731.

A revised version, whose performance was suppressed (and whose true text presumably survives in *The Grub-Street Opera*). The title of this edition protests too much: it is in fact another "bad octavo", probably printed by Rayner (some of the "comedians" disavowed the edition).

Reference: CROSS (1918), p. 293

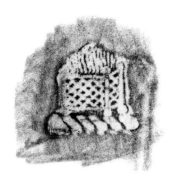
41

41. Mr. FIELDING, *The Temple Beau*. — London, 1730. Crest (rubbing): 2.3 × 2.5 cm.

Fine paper copy, without the price following the imprint; bound in original calf (rebacked), with heraldic crest (Jervays?) stamped in gilt on the front cover. Such individual bindings of plays are exceptionally rare — though one eccentric eighteenth-century owner, Lord Clinton, bound all his plays separately for his library at Bicton.

To a hitherto unrecognized extent, Fielding printed up fine paper copies of his plays, presumably for presentation; and these, of course, were individually bound. You might say that they were a kind of "offprint" from the tract volumes of plays that were the commercial norm. Like a writer contributing to a periodical, Fielding would have had very little to say about the typographical presentation of his plays.

References: CROSS (1918), p. 290 (ordinary paper copy); P.

M. Hill, Cat. 18: Bicton Library (1946), no. 297; Parke-Bernet (Herbert L. Carlebach) 20 Jan. 1948, lot 44 (this copy); MCKENZIE (1981)

42. HF, Esq., *Pasquin*. — London [i.e. Edinburgh], 1736. foolscap 8vo: [A]–H⁴ ; 62, [2] p. (p. [64] blank). 16.8 × 10.5 cm.

Unrecorded piracy. The small format betrays the origin of this reprint, probably (to judge from its ornaments) by Fleming. It could not have been neatly bound with other London properties, and therefore was not very saleable there.

Seventeenth-century English plays, sermons and pamphlets were published in quarto. Their format changed around 1700 — in London to crown octavo; elsewhere to foolscap octavo or (particularly in Ireland and America) to duodecimo. The reasons for these concerted decisions (as they must have been) are still unclear, but they indicate, as surely as a metric system, the existence of separate markets.

Reference: FEATHER (1985)

THE INVENTION OF THE ENGLISH NOVEL &

> In Truth, the Romance Writing is the only Branch of our Business now, that is worth following. Goods of that Sort have had so much Success lately in the Market, that a Bookseller scarce cares what he bids for them.
>
> *Amelia* [1751], VIII.5

> He says, that the Demand for that Species of Writing is over, or nearly so. Other Booksellers have declared the same Thing. There was a Time, when every Man of that Trade published a Novel, 'till the Public . . . became tired of them.
>
> Andrew Millar, as reported by Samuel Richardson to Lady Barbara Montagu, 17 Feb. 1759

The intellectual precedents of the novel go back to antiquity, as Fielding was well aware when he defined *Joseph Andrews* as "a comic epic in prose." To prove something like "the rise of the novel" one needs phenomena that gradually become obsolete, so that they mark the change. Intellectual phenomena don't — the epic and romance still continue to "work", even in the twentieth century. Physical evidence is ideal: its expressiveness is constantly being censored and transformed by new editions, and we forget what books "looked like" in an incredibly short time. We regularly agree that the novel is "dead" and regularly it returns to life.

43. "Monsieur" [GEORGES, or rather MADELEINE] DE SCUDERY, *Artamène, ov, Le Grand Cyrvs.* — Paris, 1650–53. 10 v., small 8vo.

Contemporary marbled boards (over half vellum); the earliest recorded set of editions (v. 1–3 are "seconde édition, reueuë & corrigée").

"Romans de longue haleine," Boileau jeered. This one is 28″ long: the multi-volume format, essential to finding your place, also establishes a more intimate relationship with the reader than folio. It is printed in *gros romain* (about 15 point) unleaded, without paragraphing — a physical correlative of the seamless interlacing of events typical of romance, perhaps?

Reference: TCHEMERZINE (1927), X, 281

44. "Monsieur" [GEORGES, or rather MADELEINE] DE SCUDERY, *Ibrahim, or, The Illvstriovs Bassa* / now englished by Henry Cogan. — London, 1652. Folio.

The normal English romance format was a small quarto; but works of any pretension (e.g., the "new" *Arcadia*, 1593) also appeared in folio, conforming them to the normal format for history; from which also derives the citation of tome and book in the headline.

45. [G. J. DE LAVERGNE, comte de GUILLERAGUES], *Lettres portvgaises* / tradvites en françois. — Paris, 1669. 12mo.

A French *nouvelle,* or short fiction; from which the English word derives. The format has shrunk, but the size of type remains the same, and the text is unparagraphed before Book 6.

Digression: Format and Type Size

The relation between type size and format is partly aesthetic, partly social, partly economic. Since the main cost of a hand-printed book is its paper, the price of an edition largely depends on the size of its type; and since small type is hard to read in long lines, cheap editions are usually in small formats or periodical format (two columns a page). Large type is socially honorific — it appears in dedications, for example, or in poetry, the "nobler" genre. These various factors make for an unstable environment, governed by two idioms (so to speak): "textualism", which associates the size of type with a given textual content; and "perspectivism", which links it with a given format.

The names of the types most commonly used in books during the eighteenth century are *long primer* (10 point), *small pica* (11 point), *pica* (12 point), *english* (13 point) and *great primer* (15 point); and the usual trade "perspectives" were quarto/english, octavo/pica, and duodecimo/small pica. The second and third perspectives are very nearly the same optical size (illus., p. 36–37).

46. [SAMUEL RICHARDSON], *Pamela, or, Virtue Rewarded* [pts. 1–2] — London, 1741 [i.e. 1740–41]. 4 v.

First editions.

The English novel before Richardson is polymorphous perverse, with no fixed format, and Richardson, a master printer, operates within this context. The duodecimo, long primer, unleaded page reflects the author's uneasy consciousness that his material had gotten out of control. "Little did I think, at first, of making one, much less two volumes of it" (to Stubbs, 2 June 1753). Even in 1753, he could not quite admit he had finally written four.

47. "CONNY KEYBER" [HF], *An Apology for the Life of Mrs. Shamela Andrews.* — London, 1741.

First edition; bound with memoirs of the actress Anne Oldfield, the actor Robert Wilks, and Queen Caroline, in contemporary blind-stamped suede, labelled on spine "LIVES".

An intellectual counterfeit of *Pamela:* it is physically indistinguishable from the other octavo pamphlets with which it is bound, whose subject (like *Shamela's*) is not literary, but journalistic. Most copies of *Shamela* have been disbound from such tract volumes, destroying evidence of the context in which they were read. For this reader, *Shamela* was just another entertaining life.

References: CROSS (1918), p. 304

48. LEWIS THEOBALD, *The History of the Loves of Antiochus and Stratonice.* — London, 1717.

One of the few typographical precedents for the idiom uniformly found in Fielding's novels: duodecimo pica, with spaced paragraphs. It was sufficiently unusual and distinctive to become the object of satire, and Fielding's success made it perhaps the commonest idiom for novels in the 1750's.

References: THORNTON (1752), p. 324

am now returning to my poor Parents again so soon, I cannot wear those good things without being whooted at; and so have bought what will be more suitable to my Degree, and be a good Holiday-suit too when I get home.

He then took me in his Arms, and presently push'd me from him. Mrs. *Jervis*, said he, take the little Witch from me; I can neither *bear*, nor *forbear* her! (Strange Words these!) --- But stay; you shan't go! ——Yet begone! ---- No, come back again.

I thought he was mad, for my Share; for he knew not what he would have. I was going, however; but he stepp'd after me, and took hold of my Arm, and brought me in again: I am sure he made my Arm black and blue; for the Marks are upon it still. Sir, Sir, said I, pray have Mercy; I will, I will come in.

He sat down, and look'd at me, and, as I thought afterwards, as sillily as such a poor Girl as I. At last, he said, Well, Mrs. *Jervis*, as I was telling you, you may permit her to stay a little longer, till I see if my Sister *Davers* will have her; if, mean time, she humble herself, and ask this as a Favour, and is sorry for her Pertness, and the Liberty she has taken with my Character, out of the House, and in the House. Your Honour indeed told me so, said Mrs. *Jervis*; but I never found her inclinable to think herself in a Fault. Pride and Perverseness, said he, with a Vengeance! Yet this is your Doating-piece! ------ Well, for once I'll submit

---

gift hath not given himself for the sake of giving the Example to his Readers.

CHAP. II.

Of Mr. Joseph Andrews *his Birth, Parentage, Education, and great Endowments; with a Word or two concerning Ancestors.*

MR. *Joseph Andrews*, the Hero of our ensuing History, was esteemed to be the only Son of Gaffar and Gammer *Andrews*, and Brother to the illustrious *Pamela*, whose Virtue is at present so famous. As to his Ancestors, we have searched with great Diligence, but little Success; being unable to trace them farther than his Great Grandfather, who, as an elderly Person in the Parish remembers to have heard his Father say, was an excellent Cudgel-player. Whether he had any Ancestors before this, we must leave to the Opinion of our curious Reader, finding nothing of sufficient Certainty to rely on. However, we cannot omit inserting an Epitaph which an ingenious Friend of ours hath communicated:

Stay Traveller, for underneath this Pew
Lies fast asleep that merry Man Andrew *;*
When the last Day's great Sun shall gild the Skies,
Then he shall from his Tomb get up and rise.
Be merry while thou canst: For surely thou
Shall shortly be as sad as he is now.

The Words are almost out of the Stone with Antiquity. But it is needless to observe, that *Andrew* here is writ without an *s*, and is besides a Christian

THE WEDDING-DAY. 15

Luc. Believe me, I could never affure myfelf of it till now ; the whole long Year that I expected his Return to *Paris*, tho' it made me fear his Falfhood, ftill left me room to hope his Truth.

Mrs. *Plot.* We are apt to hope what we defire. But could any Woman have reafon to expect the Return of a Lover, after a Month had paft beyond his Promife ? Had he intended to have married you, he would have done it before his Departure. Marriage, like Self-Murder, requires an immediate Refolution : He that takes time for Deliberation, will never accomplifh either.

Luc. Oh ! *Plotwel*, thou art well fkill'd in the Wiles of the Sex : I wonder thou couldft be deceived.

Mrs. *Plot.* Yes, Madam, I have paid for my Knowledge. Man is that forbidden Fruit which we muft buy the Knowledge of with Guilt. He muft be tafted, to be known ; and certain Poifon is in the Tafte. Were Man to appear what he really is, we fhould fly from him as from a tempeftuous Sea ; or were he to be what he appears, we fhould be happy in him as in a ferene one. They lead us into Ruin with the Face of Angels, and when the Door is fhut on us, exert the Devil.

Luc. He muft have been a Man of uncommon Senfe, who work'd your Ruin.

Mrs. *Plot.* Rather the Circumftances of my Ruin were uncommon.

Luc. I am furprifed, that in all our Acquaintance, tho' you have often mentioned your Misfortunes, you have carefully avoided entering into the Caufe of them.

Mrs. *Plot.* Tho' the Relation be uneafy to me, ftill to fatisfy your Curiofity, and to prevent any Sollicitations for the future, I will tell you in as few Words as I can.—In my Way to *Paris*, twenty Years ago, I fell acquainted with a young Gentleman, who appeared to be an Officer in the Army.
He

70: octavo, pica (83%)

49. [HF], *The History of the Adventures of Joseph Andrews.* — London, 1742. 2 v.

Unlettered calf, as issued.

This, the first edition, like *Tom Jones* and *Amelia*, is in pica; the second is in small pica, unleaded — a physical counterfeit of *Pamela*.

References: CROSS (1918), p. 305

50. [SAMUEL RICHARDSON], *Pamela, or, Virtue Rewarded.* — 6th ed. — London, 1742. 4 v.

First collected edition of both parts, with illustrations by Francis Hayman.

Pamela is one of three novels in history to go from duodecimo to octavo in the author's lifetime; the others are *Clarissa*, and *Sir Charles Grandison*, which Richardson reprinted to match, in pica. Only *Pamela* is in english — a printer's ultimate response to the "lewd ungenerous engraftments" of Fielding and others, which sullied his sense of dignity.

Reference: KREISSMAN (1960)

Wall Case

Map: European translations and dramatizations of *Tom Jones*, 1749 – 1820

51. *Arrest du Conseil d'état du Roy, qui ordonne la suppression d'un ouvrage intitulé,* Histoire de Tom Jones. — Paris, 1750.

One of two known copies; the *arrêt* was almost immediately withdrawn, but left its mark on v. 1 – 2 of the first edition of P. A. de La Place's translation, which

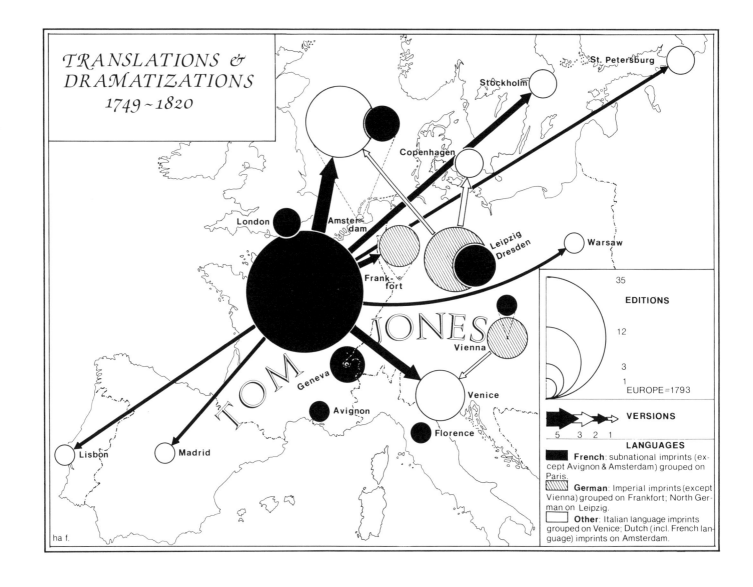

TRANSLATIONS &
DRAMATIZATIONS
1749~1820

show a mixture of sheets in two different settings. The period was one of exceptionally harsh censorship in France.

References: Rothschild 860; JONES (1961); MAY (1963)

52. HF, *Tom Jones, ou, l'Enfant trouvé* / imitation de l'anglois . . . par m. de La Place. — 4e éd. — Paris: Caillau, 1767. 4 v.

Uncut, in original blue-gray wrappers, from the library of the Counts of Holsteinborg; also issued with Bauche, Nyon, and Charpentier imprints.

This is the third revision of the translation that introduced *Tom Jones* to Europe, and for a short time elevated Fielding to the level of Shakespeare and (awful conjunction) Young. La Place abridged Fielding's introductory chapters and his continual digressions in the text, and attenuated the element of burlesque to suit Continental taste. Such translations, knows as *belles infidèles,* are interesting (or "beautiful", if you will) in direct proportion to their infidelity.

53. [HF], *Les avantures de Joseph Andrews.* — Londres {i.e. Paris?}, 1743. 2 v., 12mo: v. 1. ã⁸, ẽ⁴, A–Cc⁸·⁴, Dd⁸; v. 2. π², ã², A– Ee⁸·⁴, Ff⁴, Gg².

Second (?) edition, in original vellum.

A concealed edition of P. F. G. Desfontaines' translation. Another, possibly earlier edition (MH, CtY; ARSENAL) collates π1, ã⁸, ẽ², A–Cc⁸·⁴, Dd⁸, Ee1; π1, ã², A –Ee⁸·⁴, Ff⁴, Gg², Hh1. The presumption of priority goes to the more complex collation (it's easier to achieve a regular structure from a printed copy than from manuscript).

54. JOSEF CARL HUBER, *Der engländische Findling, oder, Die verfolgte Unschuld.* — [Wien, 1751?].

One of only two known copies.

The first published European dramatic adaptation of *Tom Jones*; it covers Books 1–6, and may be the first of a trilogy, otherwise attested only in an Italian translation.

Reference: AMORY, *"Tom Jones* in Italy" (1981)

55. HF, *Giuliano l'apostata, o sia, Viaggio nell'altro mondo.* — Livorno, 1788. (Biblioteca inglese, o sia, Scelta de'migliori romanzi del Sig. Fielding) 2 v., 12mo: v. 1. *¹², §¹², §§⁶, A–E¹², F¹⁰; v. 2 π², A–D¹² (–D4), E –H¹², ²H⁸. Opening: 16.5 × 19 cm.

Original decorated paste-paper wrappers.

Unrecorded Italian translation (as usual, from the French), with Murphy's life; showing an ink deletion by the censor (?), who also pasted leaves B6–11 (p. 35–46) in v. 1 together, to remove an episode featuring the *maladie à la mode* (syphilis).

Floor Case

56. THOMAS BIRCH, Letter to the Earl of Orrery, Jan. 1748 (copy): *"Mr. Fielding* is printing three volumes of Adventures under the title of the *Foundling."*

This and a record of some subscription receipts printed by Strahan (none of which survive) are the evidence for supposing that Fielding initially planned to publish *Tom Jones* by subscription in 3 v., presumably on

colare, giacchè eravamo obbligati di
fare la noſtra corte a differenti ma-
lattie; ed io pregai la mia guida di
condurmi dalla febbre degli spiriti
vitali; poichè era queſta la malattia
che m'aveva liberato dalla mia prigione. (2)

Passammo per molte ſtrade, e pic-
chiammo a molte porte, ma inutil-
mente; ove ci fu detto abitarvi la
consunsione; ▬▬▬▬▬▬▬▬; do-
ve l'idropisia; dove l'intemperanza,
e dove le disgrazie. Io mi ſtancava
di tante visite infruttuose, che fa-
cevano perdermi la pazienza, e nel
tempo ſtesso molto danaro, che da-

---

(2) É bene di rammemorarſi, che è ſem-
pre un'anima, o uno ſpirito che parla.

vo per dovuto riconoscimento al mio
condottiere ad ogni nuova informa-
zione; finalmente egli mi dichiarò
seriamente, che aveva fatto quanto
aveva potuto, e mi lasciò senza im-
barazzarsi di ciò che m'avverrebbe.

Subito ne rincontrai un altro, che
come il primo teneva un baſtone col
pomo d'ambra: gli usai la solita
cortesìa, e gl'indicai il nome della
malattia che cercavo. Egli pensò per
qualche minuto, e levatosi poscia
di tasca un pezzetto di carta, sul
quale scrisse qualche cosa, apparen-
temente in lingua orientale, perchè
non potei leggerla, m'ordinò di por-
tare quella carta in una certa casa
che fece osservarmi; E assicurando-
mi che troverei da compire le mie
brame, mi lasciò nell'iſtante me-
desimo.

the model of his last two efforts, the *Miscellanies* (1743) and Sarah Fielding's *Familiar Letters between the Characters of David Simple* (1747).

57. HF, Esq., *The History of Tom Jones, a Foundling*. — London, 1749. 6 v.

First edition. Vols. 1–3 were printed and circulated in advance copies by Sept. 1748; v. 6, together with the title-pages and errata for all six volumes, the preliminaries for v. 1, and two sheets of cancels (twenty-four corrected leaves), was finally published in January 1749. Four London editions (10,000 copies) and three sanctioned reprints in Dublin had appeared before the end of the year. For some reason — possibly sheer size, possibly the sanctioned Dublin editions (above, no. 21) — there were no piracies before 1767.

The first and second editions, which were published almost simultaneously, retain the idiom of *Joseph Andrews*, except that chapter headings are in pica, like the text. This seems to be a conscious choice, since we observe the same hierarchy in *Amelia*.

References: CROSS (1918), p. 316–17; WESLEYAN ED. (1975); AMORY (1977)

58. HF, Esq., *The History of Tom Jones, a Foundling*. — London, 1750 [1749]. 4 v.

Fourth London edition.
Since Fielding sold his copyright for a single lump sum, he lost control over the typography after the first edition. This reprint incorporates his revisions, but the idiom had already been set by the unauthoritative 3rd edition, a reversion to the commercial stereotype of small pica. Apart from a handful of eighteenth- and early nine-

teenth-century editions, no later reprints preserve Fielding's original tripartite structure.

Reference: CROSS (1918), p. 317–19

59. HF, Esq., *The History of Tom Jones, a Foundling*. — Paris : Didot, 1780. 4 v. t.-p.: 22.2 × 14 cm.

The first critical edition, with a title-page in the English style. Published in large and small octavo, and large and small duodecimo, for every purse. This copy is the large-paper octavo, bound in full dark green morocco, ca. 1800.

Didot collated the text of Murphy's *Works* with the text of the latest separate London edition; he offered a large-paper octavo to anyone who detected an error; and he printed the text without hyphenation, to avoid a common stumbling-block for compositors who knew no English. No copy of the large-paper duodecimo is known, but the texts of the other editions are all minutely revised.

The large-paper octavo, printed in *cicéro* (12 point), leaded, is an amazingly close approach to Fielding's original vision for his masterpiece. Its main flaws are the four-volume structure and unspaced paragraphs it inherited from the separate London edition.

Reference: Mercure de France, 10 juin 1780.

60. HF, Esq., *Amelia*. — London, 1752 [1751]; 2 copies.

The Silver copy, in blue paste-paper boards and cream paper labels, uncut (a Continental binding?); and the only known copy of the abortive "second edition", with two sheets in v. 3 reimpressed (v. 3 is correctly dated).

THE

HISTORY

OF

TOM JONES,

A

FOUNDLING.

By HENRY FIELDING, Efq;

— *Mores hominum multorum vidit* —

VOL. I.

PARIS:

Printed by Fr. Amb. Didot the eldeſt,

And ſold by { J. N. Pissot, and Barrois junior, } Bookſellers.
Quai des Auguſtins.

M. DCC. LXXX.

59

Millar had hoped that *Amelia* would repeat the success of *Tom Jones*, and according to Dr. Johnson, ordered a new impression before the first edition (5,000 copies — the largest, perhaps, of any eighteenth-century novel) was exhausted. But sales plummeted after the first day: the second Hyde copy is the only surviving physical evidence of this fiasco.

The red morocco binding on the second Hyde copy is unusual — and not just because of the *chinoiserie* of its insect motifs; few novels were ever bound in morocco. In the first copy, note how the different paper stocks produced volumes of various sizes before they were trimmed for binding.

References: CROSS (1918), p. 321–2; Sotheby (Newberry Library, ex Louis Silver) 8 Nov. 1965, lot 113; Quaritch, Cat. 885 (1967), no. 767; WESLEYAN ED. (1983)

61. *The History of Miss Emilia Beville.* — London : Printed by W. Hoggard for Francis Noble, at his Circulating Library near Middle-Row Holborn; and John Noble at his Circulating Library in St. Martin's Court, near Leicester Square, 1768. 2 v. demy 12mo.

During the 1760's and 1770's, a new idiom begins to rival Fielding's spaced paragraphs: pica leaded throughout, generally in 2 v. Its frequent appearance in the publications of the Nobles' circulating libraries probably reflects the need to stretch the limited capacities of novel writers to the capricious demand (see diagram, opposite). This *Luftroman* is about three-fifths as long as *Joseph Andrews*, and less than half the length of *Pamela*. Like other Noble imprints (all of them anonymous or pseudonymous, including one fraudulently ascribed to Fielding), it sold for three shillings a volume — the same price as Fielding's and Richardson's novels.

THE RISE (AND FALL) OF THE NOVEL
F. & J. Noble Imprints, 1750 – 1780

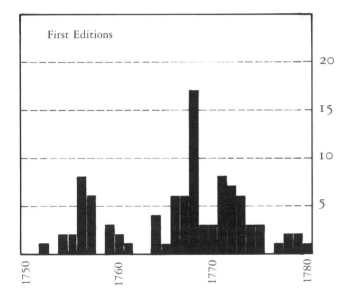

First Editions

1750   1760   1770   1780

Sources: ESTC (RLIN, 29.xi.84); C. N. Greenough Fiction Index (Houghton Library)

62. [Sir THOMAS HOPE], *Anastasius, or, Memoirs of a Greek*. — London : J. Murray, 1819. 3 v., post 8vo. Price: 31/6

Hope's work in 3 v. small pica leaded, at a half guinea a volume, is the earliest known example of an id-

iom that reigned down to 1894, the "three decker". The smaller type and finer paper only partly justify the price, which is about 175% of the market. The novel was ascribed to Byron at first — an illusion supported by the name of the publisher and perhaps its subject.

The spaciousness of the new idiom and its tripartite structure enforced Fielding's concept of the "comic epic in prose" and his Aristotelian aesthetics — in the right hands; but it also encouraged padding and melodramatic divisions — Henry James's "loose baggy monsters." Despite such criticism, the circulating libraries welcomed the new idiom: the high price encouraged borrowing, and the multi-volume format allowed multiple circulation (they also charged by the volume).

THE DESIGN OF THE MISCELLANIES

> The Volumes I now present the Public, consist, as their Title indicates, of various Matter; treating of Subjects which bear not the least Relation to each other.
>
> Pref. to the *Miscellanies.*

Wall Case

63. Demy Paper, 1811, with plastic overlay showing foolscap and crown sizes, octavo imposition, and the physical features of hand-made paper.

Improvements in the efficiency of the hand-press during the eighteenth century allowed an ever-increasing area of type to be printed per impression; so that printers adopted larger sizes of paper, moving from the foolscap usual in the seventeenth century to demy or even medium papers at the end of the eighteenth century. The folio format, like a dinosaur, became unwieldy and disappeared from common use.

References: POLLARD (1942); MCBEY (1981), no. 24

Digression: The Price of the Novel

The price of printing paper doubled between 1793 and 1801, and the cost of composition and press work rose by about a third between 1785 and 1810. These factors would adequately explain why the price of the novel doubled, but in fact it tripled during this period, and the rise was surprisingly gradual. J. M. S. Tompkins states that pages grew more crowded during the 1790's, though I have not observed it generally; the quality of paper slumped so badly that it affected press work; and one should always remember that accounting was primitive, so that publishers were not exactly aware of their costs. Characteristically, the range of prices broadened, since publishers and purchasers were simply less certain what a novel was worth (see diagram, p. 45).

Interestingly, cheap "piratical" series like Cooke's fared the worst: their margins were crowded, their print was small, their paper thin, and their competition in America and on the Continent was untaxed. Since they sold, for the most part, directly to subscribers, not to retail booksellers or circulating libraries, their demise parallels the transformation of the English public from a nation of novel-owners to one of novel-borrowers, noted by Sutherland.

None of this, however, explains why the price of the novel stabilized in the 1830's at as much as 10/6 a volume; nor why Archibald Constable and John Murray, who did not specialize in novels, priced their wares so much higher than A. K. Newman, who did.

References: Parl. Pap. (1802); ENGLISH (1894); TOMPKINS (1932); BLAKEY (1939); SUTHERLAND (1976)

Floor Case

64. PETER HEYLYN, *Aerivs Redivivvs, or, The History of the Presbyterians.* — Oxford : Printed for Jo. Crossley, and are to be sold in London, by Tho. Basset . . . and Chr. Wilkinson, 1670 [1669]; with xerox, showing a sample of the first printer's stint. 2 p.: 28 × 16 cm.

The use of multiple printers in a work of any size was common practice throughout the hand-press period; during the seventeenth century, when there were no native punch-cutters, it made uniformity difficult, The publisher here tried to disguise the "join" between the discordant type-faces and ornaments by placing a blank page at the end of the first printer's stint.

References: MADAN (1895), III, no. 2855 ("No part of the book was printed in Oxford"); MCKENZIE (1969)

65. *A Specimen by William Caslon, Letterfounder . . .,* from Ephraim Chambers, *Cyclopaedia.* — 2nd ed. — London, 1738.

Caslon, the first English punch-cutter, began to produce his romans and italics in 1724, which contributed enormously to the uniform appearance of London printing. This specimen, from a popular encyclopedia, helped writers to tell printers how they wanted their books to look.

Reference: MOSLEY (1967)

W. Lane (Minerva Press)/A. K. Newman: Novels, 1783 – 1830
Price per volume (in shillings)

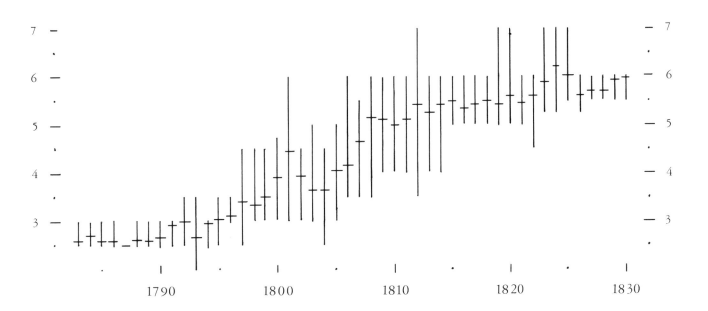

Sources: Blakey (1939); Block, 2nd ed. (1961); *London Cat.* (1835)

AERIVS REDIVIVVS:

OR,

The History

Of the

PRESBYTERIANS.

LIB. IV.

Containing

Their beginning, Progress and Positions; their dangerous Practices, Insurrections, and Conspiracies in the Realm of Scotland, from the year 1544 to the year 1566.

1. **C**Ross we next over into *Scotland*, where the *Genevian* Principles were first reduced into use and practice. In which respect the *Presbyterians* of that Realm should have had precedencie in the present story, not only before any of their Brethren in the *Belgick* Provinces, but even before the *French* themselves, though nearest both in scituation and affection to the Mother-City. For though the Emissaries of *Geneva* had long been tampering with that active and unquiet people; yet such a strict hand was held upon them both by *Francis* the First, and *Henry* the Second his Successor, that they durst not stir, till by the death of those two Kings they found the way more free and open to pursue those counsels, which by the industry of those men had been put into them, before which time the *Scots* had acted over all those Tumults, Riots and Rebellions, in which not long after they were followed by the *French* and *Netherlands*. But howsoever I have purposely

T 2   posely

AERIVS REDIVIVVS:

OR,

The History

OF THE

PRESBYTERIANS.

LIB. VIII.

Containing

The Seditious Practises and Positions of the English Puritans, *their Libels, Railing, and Reviling, in order to the setting up of the Holy Discipline, from the year* 1584, *to the year* 1589. *The undutiful Carriage of the* French, *and the horrible Insolencies of the* Scotch *Presbyters, from the year* 1585, *to the year* 1592.

Aving thus prosecuted the Affairs of the *Presbyterians* in *England*, to the same point of time where before we left the *Scots*, the *French*, and those of the same Party in the *Belgick* Provinces: we shall hereafter treat of them as they come before us with reference to the Practises and Proceedings of their *English* Brethren. And first, beginning with the *Scots*, it is to be remembred, that we left them at a very low ebb; the Earl of *Goury* put to death, many of the Nobility exiled into Forreign Countreys, and the chief Zealots of the Faction amongst the Ministers, putting themselves into a voluntary Banishment, because they could not have their wills on the King and Council.

1584.

Aaa   *England,*

66. ROBERT SOUTH, *Twelve Sermons.* — 3rd ed. — London, 1715. 20 × 11.5 cm.

One of four collections with the same title, making a multivolume unit with the unimaginative general title of *Forty-Eight Sermons.* The ferociously handsome page represents an innovation: the use of english for prose, in octavo. Earlier, seventeenth-century editions, predictably, were in folio.

There were no book designers in the eighteenth century. Either you gave the printer a sample (so Sterne specified that *Tristram Shandy* should look like *Rasselas*); or you ordered trial proofs until you got the effect you wanted (as Boswell and Malone did for *The Life of Johnson*, and probably as South did here).

References: STERNE, *Letters,* to Dodsley [Oct. 1759]; BOSWELL PAPERS, XVII, 7

67. ROBERT SOUTH, *Twelve Sermons.* — 6th ed. — London, 1727. 20 × 11.5 cm.

A page-for-page reprint of the earlier edition by William Bowyer, who also printed v. 3 of Fielding's *Miscellanies.* The increased leading is the most conspicuous change, but note also the two-line initials, italic great primer drop titles, and twin-rule headers — all features that will also be found in the *Miscellanies.* Only one other prose octavo in english, leaded is known before the *Miscellanies* — Elizabeth Rowe's *Devout Exercises of the Heart* (1737). Fielding's known predilection for South makes this a very likely model for his later work — though he owned a copy of the 5th edition, which is typographically closer to the third.

Reference: BAKER SALE (1755), no. 46

MATTHEW X. 33.

But whosoever shall deny me before Men, him will I deny before my Father which is in Heaven.

S the great comprehensive Gospel-Duty is the Denial of Self, so the grand Gospel Sin that confronts it, is the Denial of Christ. These Two are both the commanding and the dividing Principles of all our Actions : For whosoever acts in Opposition to one, does it always in behalf of the other. None ever opposed Christ, but it was to gratify Self : None ever renounced the Interest of Self, but from a prevailing Love to the Interest of Christ. The Subject I have here pitched upon, may seem improper in these Times, and in this Place, where the Number of Professors, and of Men, is the same ; where the Cause and Interest of

G 2   Christ

(85)

MATTHEW X. 33.

But whofoever fhall deny me before Men, him will I deny before my Father which is in Heaven.

AS the great comprehenfive Gofpel Duty is the Denial of Self, fo the grand Gofpel Sin that confronts it, is the Denial of Chrift. Thefe Two are both the commanding and the dividing Principles of all our Actions : For whofoever acts in Oppofition to one, does it always in behalf of the other. None ever oppofed Chrift, but it was to gratify Self : None ever renounced the Intereft of Self, but from a prevailing Love to the Intereft of Chrift. The Subject I have here pitched upon, may feem improper in thefe Times, and in this Place, where the Number of Profeffors, and of Men, is the fame ; where the Caufe and Intereft of

G 2   Chrift

68. *Miscellany Poems* / [ed. John Dryden]. — London, 1684.

For poetry, the typographical idiom was (and still is) different. This famous collection is set in english, leaded — not unusual, for poetry, even in octavo. It can do this without many "turn ups" (overrun lines) because the type has a relatively narrow "set", compared to Caslon's english.

This is another precedent that would inevitably have occurred to Fielding, but one he failed to follow in the poetic parts of his collection, which are set in pica.

69. HF, Esq., *Miscellanies*. — London : Printed for the Author, and sold by A. Millar, 1743. 3 v. 2 p.: 20.5 × 11.5 cm.

The Kern copy, uncut, in trade half sheep and marbled boards; the absence of the subscribers' list in v. 1, and the binding — reported to be characteristic of Millar's publications — argue that this is a late issue of sheets; Millar's successors still had them for sale in 1775.

The *Miscellanies* were set by three printers: William Strahan (v. 1); Henry Woodfall the elder (v. 2); and William Bowyer (v. 3). Volume 1 is in pica, 30 lines to the page, because it contains the poetry; vols. 2 – 3, in prose, are in english, 27 lines to the page. All three volumes observe Fielding's augmented paragraphing, and vols. 2 – 3 observe the same hierarchy: three-line initials for books; two-line initials for chapters; chapter titles in italic great primer, with the second half-line centered, otherwise with hanging indent.

This sort of thing does not happen by chance; in a privately published book like the *Miscellanies,* we must assign responsibility to the author. And it is a character-

A

JOURNEY, &c.

BOOK XIX.

CHAP. VII.

Wherein Anna Boleyn *relates the History of her Life.*

'IAM going now truly to recount a Life,
'which from the Time of its ceasing,
'has been, in the other World, the con-
'tinual Subject of the Cavils of contending
'Parties ; the one making me as black as Hell,
'the other as pure and innocent as the Inhabi-
'tants of this blessed Place ; the Mist of Pre-
'judice blinding their Eyes, and Zeal for
'what they themselves profess, making every
'thing appear in that Light, which they think
'most conduces to its Honour.

'   'My

THE

HISTORY

OF THE

LIFE of the late

Mr. JONATHAN WILD the Great.

BOOK III.

CHAP. I.

The low and pitiful Behaviour of Heartfree; *and the foolish Conduct of his Apprentice.*

HIS Misfortunes did not entirely prevent *Heartfree* from closing his
Eyes. On the contrary, he slept
several Hours the first Night of his Con-
finement. However, he perhaps paid too
severely

istic expression of his genius: the typographical degradation of poetry is mock-epic; the exaggerated paragraphs are mock-romance.

References: CROSS (1918), p. 308–9; Anderson (Jerome Kern), 7 Jan. 1929, lot 510

Digression: Letter-size and Letter Space

We see a letter on the printed page together with (or as an expression of) an imaginary rectangle that it occupies; so that leading makes a letter look larger. Compare the generously spaced Latin (about 23 lines per page) with the English (30 lines per page) in the *Miscellanies,* v. 1 (illus.). This solution to the social need for typographical grandeur is relatively economical, since more text can be fitted in per line than would be the case if it were printed in larger type, set solid—as is characteristic of seventeenth-century typography (cf. Guilleragues, no. 45 above). It also illustrates the eighteenth-century predilection for a literal "enlightenment": more and more white space, lighter faces, and finally the reduction of ascenders by the elimination of initial capitals (1750) and the long *s* (1780). The use of "black letter" was eventually confined to the printing of the statutes, and even there to public acts.

Reference: LAUFER (1984)

70. HF, Esq., *The Wedding-Day.* — London, 1743; 2 copies, showing press variants.

No two copies of a hand-printed book are likely to be the same. These two show Fielding removing dashes after final punctuation, and they point in two directions: back to a manuscript in which the dash signalled a change of speaker (a common convention in Fielding's novels); forward to the *Miscellanies,* which was printing at the same time as this edition, and in which Fielding carried his elimination of the compositor's misunderstandings still further. Fielding made practically no revisions of the wording of the text, apart from the correction of typos.

Reference: CROSS (1918), p. 308

71. HF, "The Wedding-Day", in the *Miscellanies : v. 2.* — 2nd ed. — London : Printed for A. Millar, 1743.

The "2nd ed." of the *Miscellanies* is merely a press-variant t.-p. — a fairly common device for moving stock at a time when t.-p.'s had to do double duty as blurb. Though it is sometimes supposed that the variant imprint served to distinguish the copies Millar published on his own account from those that Fielding delivered to the subscribers, surviving copies show a thorough mixture of the two "editions", which should therefore be seen as different states, not different issues.

The change from pica, unleaded, to english, leaded, is explosive with significance, a liberation from commercial convention; it expresses exactly what Fielding meant by "good nature"—the expansive *beau geste* that all too often he could not afford.

72. HF, Esq., *Of True Greatness.* — London, 1741.

This is unusual only because it is so normal: Fielding's only separately published poem in the folio conventional for poetry—negligent of space, as became the noblest genre, and cumbersome to read, but so what? His other efforts were more practical affairs: *The Corona-*

JUVENALIS
SATYRA
SEXTA.

CRedo pudicitiam Saturno rege moratam
In terris, visamque diu ; cùm frigida parvas
Præberet spelunca domos, ignemque, Laremque,
Et pecus, & dominos communi clauderet umbrâ :
Silvestrem montana torum cùm sterneret uxor
Frondibus & culmo, vicinarumque ferarum

N O T Æ.

Saturno Rege. Aureo scilicet sæculo ; quod viguisse Saturno,
Cœli et Vestæ filio, in Latio regnante a Poetis fingitur. Regem
hunc eleganter satis Poeta profert, cum de moribus in Latio mu-
atis agitur.
Vicinarumque. Contubernalium. Vel forsan non longe peti-
tarum sicut nunc ; et exprobrare vult sui Temporis Romanis,
qui ex longinquo, mollitiei vel odoris causâ, Ferarum pelles maxi-
mo cûm pretio comparabant.

Pellibus :

PART OF
Juvenal's Sixth SATIRE,
MODERNIZED IN
BURLESQUE VERSE.

DAME *Chastity*, without Dispute,
   Dwelt on the Earth with good King *Brute* ;
When a cold Hut of modern *Greenland*
Had been a Palace for a Queen *Anne* ;
When hard and frugal Temp'rance reign'd,
And Men no other House contain'd
Than the wild Thicket, or the Den ;
When Houshold Goods, and Beasts, and Men,
Together lay beneath one Bough,
Which Man and Wife would scarce do now ;
The Rustick Wife her Husband's Bed
With Leaves and Straw, and Beast-Skin made.

N O T E S.

King Brute. The *Roman* Poet mentions *Saturn*, who was
the first King of *Italy* ; we have therefore rendered *Brute* the
oldest to be found in our Chronicles, and whose History is as
fabulous as that of his *Italian* Brother.

Not

314 *The LIFE of* Book IV.
" which the Blood of Millions cannot
" wipe away! Was it only that the
" few, the fimple Part of Mankind,
" fhould call me a *Rogue*, perhaps I could
" fubmit; but to be for ever contemptible
" to the *PRIGS*, as a Wretch who want-
" ed Spirit to execute my Undertaking,
" can never be digefted. What is the Life
" of a fingle Man? Have not whole Ar-
" mies and Nations been facrificed to the
" Humour of *ONE GREAT MAN?*
" Nay, to omit that firft Clafs of GREAT-
" NESS, the Conquerors of Mankind, how
" often have Numbers fallen, by a ficti-
" tious Plot, only to fatisfy the Spleen, or
" perhaps exercife the Ingenuity of a
" Member of that fecond Order of
" GREATNESS the *Minifterial!* What have
" I done then? Why, I have ruined a Fa-
" mily, and brought an innocent Man to
" the Gallows. I ought rather to weep,
" with *Alexander*, that I have ruined no
" more, than to regret the little I have
" done." He at length, therefore, brave-
ly refolved to confign over *Heartfree* to his
Fate, though it coft him more ftrug-
gling than may eafily be believed, utterly
to

tion (1727), known only from an advertisement and possi-
bly suppressed; *The Masquerade* (1728), surviving in five
copies (CtY; ST. DAVID'S LAMPETER, BLICKLING HALL;
W. H. Robinson, Cat. 60 (1936), no. 73; Parke-Bernet
(Herbert L. Carlebach), 20 Jan. 1948, lot 41); and *The
Vernoniad* (1741), both in small quarto.

References: CROSS (1918), p. 302–3 (describing a copy of
the 1755 reprint); FOXON F123

73. HF, "Of True Greatness", in the *Miscellanies : v. 1.* — 2nd ed. — London, 1743.

This poor pica is what poetry was reduced to in Fielding's ideal book: a state of mendicancy.

74. HF, Esq., *The Life of Mr. Jonathan Wild the
Great.* — London, 1743. (The Miscellanies ; v. 3). 20.2 × 12 cm.

This is the closest Fielding ever got to an ideal
expression for a novel — apart from his sister's *Familiar
Letters between the Characters of David Simple* (1747), which
uses just the same layout and was also published by subscription. The leading gives room for much expressive typographical play: GREAT MAN, and other gestures in
small capitals recur like red flags throughout.

75. HF, Esq., *The Life of Mr. Jonathan Wild the
Great.* — New ed. — London, 1754; 12mo.
Bookplate (platemark): 9.5 × 6.2 cm.

Millar apparently planned this edition as "VOL. I." of
a series (cf. the signature title), conceivably a collection
of Fielding's novels; but nothing came of it. In this state,

the author's name is correctly spelled on the t.-p.; another state reads *FEILDING*.

Fielding, now a supporter of the ministry, reduced his typographical and textual burlesque and generalized his satire: "Statesman" regularly replaces the loaded "Prime Minister" and GREAT MAN loses its small capitals. But we don't have to read this conformist small pica very closely to see that Fielding's satire has lost its edge; in his last work, with his dying breath, he even found heart to praise Walpole.

The Spixworth Park copy, with the label of Charles Whibley (a later owner). This extensive country library, rich in novels and plays, was formed by Francis Longe (1748–1812), who inserted an engraved plate (illustrated) and stamped his crest on the covers of the books. 325 tract-volumes of plays from this source went to the Library of Congress in 1908; the remainder of the library was sold in Norwich, from which a selection appears in Dobell, Cat. 207 (July 1912), p. 38–39.

References: CROSS (1918), p. 325–6 (variant state); S. Mealey Mills, Norwich: Spixworth Park, 14 Mar. 1912 (copy in the Norwich Central Libraries)

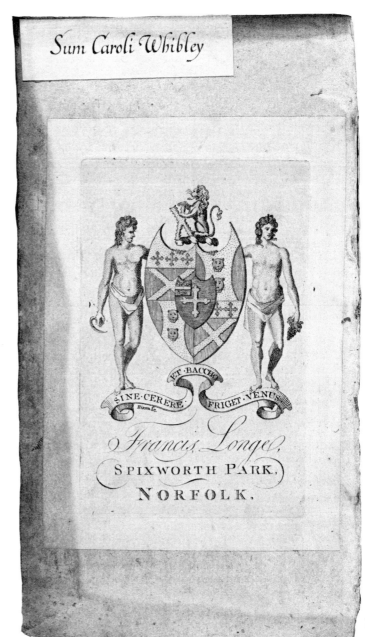

SHORT REFERENCES

Note: Library symbols are those used in Wing (for British libraries) and the pre-1956 NUC (for America). I have tried to explain bibliographical terms as they occurred in the text, but the reader may wish to consult John Carter, *ABC for Book Collectors* (5th ed., 1972) if I have not adequately met his or her needs.

AMORY (1968)   Hugh Amory, "A Preliminary Census of Henry Fielding's Legal Manuscripts," *Papers of the Bib. Soc. of America* 62 (1968), 587.

AMORY, "Criminal Legislation" (1971)   ———, "Henry Fielding and the Criminal Legislation of 1751–52," *Philological Quarterly* 50 (1971), 175.

AMORY, "Lisbon Letters" (1971)   ———, "Fielding's Lisbon Letters," *Huntington Library Quarterly* 35 (1971), 65.

AMORY (1977)   ———, "*Tom Jones* Plus and Minus," *Harvard Lib. Bull.* 25 (1977), 101.

AMORY, "First Recension" (1981)   ———, "Andrew Millar and the First Recension of Fielding's *Works* (1762)," *Trans. Cambridge Bib. Soc.* 8 (1981), 57.

AMORY, "*Tom Jones* in Italy" (1981)   ———, "*Tom Jones* in Italy," *Harvard Lib. Bull.* 29 (1981), 44.

AMORY (1984)   ———, " '*De facto* Copyright?' " *Eighteenth Century Studies* 17 (1983), 449.

ARNOTT   James F. Arnott and J. W. Robinson, *English Theatrical Literature, 1559–1900* (London, 1970).

BAKER (1959)   Sheridan Baker, "Henry Fielding's *The Female Husband*," *PMLA* 74 (1959), 213.

BAKER SALE (1755)   Samuel Baker (Henry Fielding), 10 Feb. 1755, in A. N. L. Munby (gen. ed.) *Sales Catalogues of Libraries of Eminent Persons* VII (London 1973).

BATTESTIN (1983)   Martin C. Battestin, "Pictures of Fielding," *Eighteenth Century Studies* 17 (1983/84), [1].

BATTESTIN (1986)   ———, "Fielding's Contributions to the *Universal Spectator* (1736–7)," *Studies in Philology* 83 (1986), 88.

BATTESTINS (1978)   M. C. with R. R. Battestin, "Fielding, Bedford, and the Westminster Election of 1749," *Eighteenth Century Studies* 11 (1977/78), 143.

BATTESTINS (1980)   ———, "A Fielding Discovery, with some Remarks on the Canon," *Studies in Bibliography* 33 (1980), [131].

Bibliotheca (1983)   *Bibliotheca* / Friends of the Library of the University of Pennsylvania, 1, no. 3 (Sum. 1983).

BLAKEY (1939)   Dorothy Blakey, *The Minerva Press, 1790–1820* (London, 1939).

BOCHER (1882)   Emmanuel Bocher, *Jean Michel Moreau le jeune. Les gravures françaises du XVIIIe siècle*, fasc. 6 (Paris, 1882).

BOSWELL PAPERS   *The Private Papers of Boswell from Malahide Castle in the Collection of Lt.-Col. R. H. Isham* (Mt. Vernon, N.Y., 1928–34).

BRONSON (1958)   Bertrand H. Bronson, *Printing as an Index of Taste in Eighteenth Century England* (New York, 1958).

CLEARY (1984)   Thomas R. Cleary, *Henry Fielding, Political Writer* (Waterloo, Ont., 1984).

COHN (1924)   Albert Mayer Cohn, *George Cruikshank* (London, 1924).

CRESSY (1980)   David Cressy, *Literacy and the Social Order* (Cambridge, 1980).

CROSS (1918)   Wilbur L. Cross, "Bibliography," in *The History of Henry Fielding*, v. 3 (New Haven, 1918), [287]–366.

ELIAS (1984)   A. C. Elias, Jr., "Scribleriana Transferred," *The Scriblerian* 17 (1984), 79.

ENGLISH (1894)   R. English, "The Price of the Novel," *The Author* (London) 5 (1894), 94.

EVANS   Charles Evans et al., *American Bibliography, 1639–1800* (Chicago, 1903–34); with Supplement by R. P. Bristol (Charlottesville, Va., 1970).

FEATHER (1981)   John Feather, "John Nourse and his Authors," *Studies in Bibliography* 34 (1981), 205.

FEATHER (1985)   ———, *The Provincial Book Trade in Eighteenth-Century England* (Cambridge, 1985).

Four Oaks (1967)   *Four Oaks Library,* ed. Gabriel Austin (Somerville, N.J., 1967).

FOXON, *Lyell Lectures* (1975)   D. F. Foxon, "Pope and the Early Eighteenth-Century Book-Trade." Lyell Lectures (1975)—typescript at the Bodleian.

FOXON   ———, *English Verse 1701–1750* (Cambridge, 1975).

GASKELL (1972)   Philip Gaskell, *A New Introduction to Bibliography* (New York, 1972).

GEORGE (1929)   M. D. George, "The Early History of Registry Offices," *Economic Journal* 1, Supp. (Jan. 1929), 570.

GILREATH (1986)   James Gilreath, "American Book Distribution," *Proc. of the American Antiquarian Soc.* 95 (1986), 501.

GREEN (1902)   Emanuel Green, *Bibliotheca Somersetensis* (Taunton, 1902).

HONAN (1960)   Park Honan, "Eighteenth and Nineteenth Century English Punctuation Theory," *English Studies* (Amsterdam) 41 (1960), 92.

HOWE (1947)   Ellic Howe, *The London Compositor* (London, 1947).

JARVIS (1945)   R. C. Jarvis, "Fielding, Dodsley, Marchant and Ray," *Notes & Queries* n.s. 8 (1945), 90, 117, 138.

JARVIS (1946)   ———, "The Death of Walpole," *Modern Lang. Rev.* 41 (1946), 113.

JENSEN (1935)   Gerard E. Jensen, "A Fielding Discovery," *Yale Univ. Lib. Gazette* 10 (1935), 23.

KREISSMAN (1960)   Bernard Kreissman, *Pamela-Shamela* ([Lincoln, Neb.], 1960).

JONES (1961)   B. P. Jones, "Was There a Temporary Suppression of *Tom Jones* in France?" *Modern Lang. Notes* 76 (1961), 495.

LANGBEIN, "Fatal Flaws" (1983)   John H. Langbein, "Albion's Fatal Flaws," *Past & Present* 98 (1983), [96].

LANGBEIN, "Trial" (1983)   ———, "Shaping the Eighteenth-Century Criminal Trial," *Univ. of Chicago Law Rev.* 50 (1983), 1.

LAUFER (1984)   Roger Laufer, "Les espaces du livre," in *Histoire de l'édition française* II ([Paris], 1984).

LIESENFELD (1984)   Vincent J. Liesenfeld, *The Licensing Act of 1737* (Madison, 1984).

LINEBAUGH (1975)   Peter Linebaugh, "The Tyburn Riot against the Surgeons," in *Albion's Fatal Tree* (New York, 1975).

LOCKWOOD (1980)   Thomas Lockwood, "A New Essay by Fielding," *Modern Philology* 78 (1980), 48.

LOCKWOOD (1986)   *The History of Our Own Times (1741)*, ed. Thomas Lockwood (New York, 1986).

LONSDALE (1979)   Roger Lonsdale, "New Attributions to John Cleland," *Rev. of English Studies* n.s. 20 (1979), 271.

MADAN (1895)   Falconer Madan, *Oxford Books*, 3 v. (Oxford, 1895–1931).

MAY (1963)   Georges May, *Le dilemme du roman au XVIIIe siècle* (New Haven, 1963).

MCBEY (1981)   *The James McBey Collection of Watermarked Paper* (Cambridge, Mass., 1981).

MCKENZIE (1969)   D. F. McKenzie, "Printers of the Mind," *Studies in Bibliography* 22 (1969), 1.

MCKENZIE (1981)   ———, "Typography and Meaning," in *Buch und Buchhandel in Europa im achtzehnten Jahrhundert* (Hamburg, 1981), p. [81] (Wolfenbütteler Schriften zur Geschichte des Buchwesens, Bd. 4).

MORISSEY (1973)   Henry Fielding, *The Grub-Street Opera,* ed. L. J. Morissey (Edinburgh, 1973).

MOSLEY (1967)   James Mosley, "The Early Career of William Caslon," *Journal of the Printing Historical Soc.* 3 (1967), [66].

NERBONNE (1978)   Joseph J. Nerbonne, "Book Pirating is Lively on Formosa, but Authorized Reprints are Making Gains," *Publishers Weekly* (7 Aug. 1978), p. 28.

OSSELTON (1985)   N. E. Osselton, "Spelling-Book Rules and the Capitalization of Nouns in the Seventeenth and Eighteenth Centuries," in *Historical & Editorial Studies in Medieval & Early Modern English, for Johan Gerritsen,* ed. Mary-Jo Arn et al. (Groningen, 1985), p. 49.

Parl. Pap. (1802)   Great Britain, Parliament. *Report from the Committee on the Booksellers and Printers Petition, 22 Mar. 1802* (Sessional Papers [1801–2], II, 89).

PAULSON (1965)   Ronald Paulson, *Hogarth's Graphic Works,* 2 v. (New Haven, 1965).

PHILLIPS (1952)   James W. Phillips, "A Bibliographical Enquiry into Printing and Bookselling in Dublin, 1670 to 1800," Trinity College, Dublin, Ph.D. Thesis (1952).

POLLARD (1942)   H. G. Pollard, "Notes on the Size of the Sheet," *Library,* 4th ser. 22 (1942), [105].

POLLARD (1956)   ———, "Changes in the Style of Bookbinding, 1550–1830," *Library,* 5th ser. 11 (1956), 71.

RANDALL (1935)   David A. Randall, "Waverly in America," *Colophon* n.s. 1 (1935).

Rothschild   *The Rothschild Library* (Cambridge, 1954).

SCRAGG (1974)   D. G. Scragg, *A History of English Spelling* (Manchester, 1974).

SPUFFORD (1981)   Margaret Spufford, *Small Books and Pleasant Histories* (London, 1981).

STERNE, *Letters*   Laurence Sterne, *Letters,* ed. Curtis (Oxford, 1945, repr. 1965).

SUTHERLAND (1976)   J. A. Sutherland, *Victorian Novelists and Publishers* (London, 1976).

TAYLOR (1960)   Robert H. Taylor, *Letters of English Authors* [Princeton, N. J., 1960].

TCHEMERZINE (1927)   Avenir Tchemerzine, *Bibliographie d'éditions originales et rares d'auteurs français des XVe, XVIe, XVIIe et XVIIIe siècles* (Paris, 1927–34).

THORNTON (1752)   [Bonnell Thornton], *Have At You All* (13 Feb. 1752), reprinted in *Henry Fielding: The Critical Heritage,* ed. R. Paulson & T. Lockwood (London, 1969).

TOMPKINS (1932)   J. M. S. Tompkins, *The Popular Novel in England, 1770–1800* (London, 1932; repr. Lincoln, Neb., 1961).

TREADWELL (1982)   Michael Treadwell, "London Trade Publishers 1675–1750," *Library,* 6th ser. 4 (1982), [99].

WESLEYAN ED.   *The Wesleyan Edition of the Works of Henry Fielding* (Middletown, Conn., 1967–   ).

ZIRKER (1966)   Malvin R. Zirker, *Fielding's Social Pamphlets* (Berkeley, 1966).